Preaching the gospel is a God-given task to be undertaken by those men who have the knowledge and ability to communicate to the hearts of men the mind and will of God.

Preaching certainly needs to be biblically sound in its content and ably delivered. But nothing is more critical to success in declaring this life-transforming message than the godly character of the one proclaiming it. Preaching is not a profession but a function of being a disciple of Jesus. The most important thing about those who preach is not that they are preachers but that they are devoted Christians. That certainly is the ideal but there is no myth so widely held as the idea that those who spend their lives preaching the gospel are somehow insulated from the temptations that assault other disciples. To the contrary it may be true to say that they are confronted by it even more. **Behind the Preacher's Door** is a book that faces this reality squarely and candidly and offers both warning and wise counsel in meeting and overcoming the challenges with which preachers struggle. This is a book that has been long needed and we commend Warren Berkley and his writers for their diligent work in producing it. Preachers young and old will read it with great profit.

– Paul Earnhart

BEHIND THE PREACHER'S DOOR

Edited by Warren Berkley

Published by
Spiritbuilding Publishing
15591 N. State Rd. 9, Summitville, IN 46070

Spiritual "equipment" for the contest of life.
Printed in the United States of America

Behind The Preacher's Door, edited by Warren Berkley
ISBN: 9780982137680

www.Spiritbuilding.com

Cover Design by Erin Sullivan

Acknowledgements

I am mindful of so many people who have united to get this book into your hands. My initial ideas about the project were refined and supplemented by Mark Roberts and Carl McMurray. Our writers worked under brutal deadlines, yet have turned out first-rate material. Erin Sullivan did the proofreading for me in less than two weeks, bringing a professional quality of excellence to the final product. My wife, Paula, has supplied encouragement to all my work for 40 years. Thanks to those who read the pre-publication manuscript when I needed a fresh set of eyes. Also the people at **Spiritbuilding** surround Carl with skills and efficiency visible in their products. Faithful Christians have formed a vibrant little unit to get this book into circulation. They are worthy of my praise.

– Warren E. Berkley

Contents

Why This Book?
Warren E. Berkley

Speaking to a group of young preachers a few years ago, I gave them a sad review from my own personal knowledge of preachers who had fallen. At the time I had been preaching for 38 years (5 churches, over 100 gospel meetings, work outside the country in two locations, over 30 years experience in "brotherhood journalism," and contact with many preachers through **Expository Files** and **Preceptor**). I had to report to these young men that I personally knew of 52 preachers who committed sexual immorality. That's just one of the problems addressed in this book.

Adding Some Perspective: *I've known 4 men to leave the truth for Calvinism; 3 to embrace what I believe is error on divorce and remarriage; 2 to change directions into the institutional movement; 4 whose wives left them; 3 who suffered financial crash (with legal trouble); 1 who was too discouraged and depressed to continue in local work; 1 who committed suicide; 2 who just quit serving the Lord, and other sad stories.* But beyond these, 52 who fell into sexual sin (I spoke to those young preachers about this in 2008, I must now add two more). **That's 54!**

But that figure is not *just* 54 preachers. *This figure translates into at least 54 local churches, 108 families,* and I don't want to calculate how many children, parents, extended family, friends, and other churches have been hit hard by the sin of these preachers. And sadly, in some communities these episodes have been covered by local news media. In one case, the national news media exposed the transgression. The rate of such events is alarming, even when we factor in the most optimistic realities that this is a guilty minority. [As Frank Jamerson reminds us, "...the vast majority are diligently trying to teach the truth and exemplify it in their lives."]

Outside of our brethren, you'll hear reports of 1,500 "pastors" leaving "the ministry" due to moral failure. One source says that 50% of "pastor's marriages will end in divorce," and "almost 40 percent report that they have had an extra-marital affair since beginning their ministry." Shall we try and convince ourselves that we are so different from the world? We should be.

(Sources:http://blog.worldvillage.com/society/reframing_pastor_burnout_and_
pastors_leaving_ministry.html; http://www.religioustolerance.org/chr_dira.htm.)

There is a problem. Preachers need to face it; those who train preachers need to attend to it; in fact all Christians need to see the matter clearly and uphold and model the discipline that is so greatly needed. Preachers need to talk about it – not as gossip but as reality, an issue to be addressed through a faithful use of the Word. All of us striving for purity need a book like this, but most importantly, men just beginning to preach need to have this kind of book and give healthy thought to the varied content of these chapters.

So this is NOT a book about how to prepare sermons, pulpit dynamics, study methods or the use of PowerPoint. While all of these things play a role in the preacher's public work, there are books and venues directed to these purposes. ***This book is about what happens behind the preacher's door.*** These chapters put the spotlight on heart, life, private thoughts and relationships, using the Bible to teach and warn all preachers and all Christians. It is the purpose of this book to not only sound some alarms, but to supply forceful preventive teaching. You will read not only about adultery, but financial crisis, wasted time, neglect of family, and abuse of brethren. Everything Paul warned Timothy to shun!

Why this book? To apply Bible teaching to help preachers, and others, train their conscience, heighten their awareness of temptation, enrich their daily discipline, and become men of God in and out of the pulpit. Even the mass of good faithful men will be better equipped and enabled to meet future temptation by reviewing the teaching on these pages.

Foreword
Frank Jamerson

One of the brothers of our Lord wrote, "My brethren, let not many of you become teachers, knowing that we shall receive a stricter judgment" (James 3:1). We know that God is no respecter of persons and He does not classify sins as being worse if they are committed by preachers, but we should realize that those of us who publicly proclaim God's word have a special responsibility to exemplify what we teach. Teachers, by the very nature of their work, have greater opportunities to say one thing and practice another. The apostle Paul wrote concerning his Jewish brethren, "You who say, 'Do not commit adultery', do you commit adultery? You who abhor idols, do you rob temples? You who make your boast in the law, do you dishonor God through breaking the law?" (Romans 2:20-22). Then he concluded that God's name was blasphemed among the Gentiles because of the action of those who claimed to be God's people (verse 24). I have heard it said, if you can't preach better than you can practice, you are not worth listening to, but brethren, if we don't try to practice what we preach, we are not fit to listen to. A hypocrite is not simply one who makes mistakes, but one who is a play-actor. He is pretending to be what he is not, and Jesus described such action as "whitewashed tombs which indeed appear beautiful outwardly, but inside are full of dead men's bones and all uncleanness" (Matthew 23:27). Not a very pretty picture!

It has been my privilege to read the manuscripts of this book and make some comments about the various problems faced by preachers that are discussed in it. Some of these problems were unknown to those of us in the older generation, but we live in a new age, and need to be warned about new dangers as well as the old ones that have always assaulted God's servants. Instant communication can be good or evil, and it is often used for the latter. These men, who have been asked to write various chapters have not written from a spirit of self-righteousness but from genuine concern over the loss of so many comrades. You will find everything from planning time for personal spiritual growth to preparing lessons; teaching on moral purity and friendship with the local church and special friends; dangers and benefits of technology available to us, as well as the advantages and disadvantages of being married and the responsibilities to our wives and families if we are married. All the men have presented Scriptural teaching as well as beneficial lessons from their personal experiences and wisdom.

No doubt, none of our brethren who have fallen ever thought it would happen to them. When we are deceived into thinking Paul's admonition, "let him who thinks he stands take heed lest he fall" (1 Corinthians 10:12), does not apply to us, we let down our guard and the devil seizes the opportunity to take advantage of our over-confidence.

Young men, especially, need to be warned about putting themselves in a position to be tempted, or to even be accused of impropriety. Several young men have worked with me through the years and one thing that I tried to impress on them is not to take chances with their reputation. Keep the door closed for temptation, by never going behind a closed door alone with a woman, even if you do not foresee any problem. If you avoid the possibility of temptation, you will avoid being overcome by it. Society today is not the same as it was when many of us were young preachers and we must train our young men to "abstain from every form of evil" (1 Thessalonians 5:22), and as much as possible, even from the opportunities to do evil, or to be falsely accused.

As you read these chapters, you will probably think, as I did, that this kind of teaching should have been published long ago. Not only preachers, but all Christians can benefit from the excellent articles these men have written. They have warned not only about being overtaken in a trespass, but the attitude we should have when overtaken, and the attitude we should have toward those who have been overtaken. Too many times, when preachers, who have faithfully served God for years, are overcome in some sinful action, they become embittered, because they feel brethren have not treated them the way they should have been treated when they repented, and bitterness breeds all kinds of rationalizations which enable them to teach and practice things they would have never considered otherwise. In reading this book, we should remember that mistakes can make us bitter or better, depending on our reaction. Being mistreated does not justify destruction of previous good, or failure to do great things for God in the future. Remember that at one point Peter said, "even if all are made to stumble because of You, I will never be made to stumble" (Matthew 26:33). Satan took advantage of his overconfidence and Peter denied his Lord three times. When the rooster crowed, "Peter remembered the word of Jesus who had said to him, 'Before the rooster crows, you will deny Me three times.' Then he went out and wept bitterly" (Matthew 26:75). The lesson we need to learn is that he did not become bitter because of his failure. Bitterness destroys its victim. Peter got up and started over by earning the respect of his fellow apostles, and we remember him as the great evangelist, who stood with the other apostles on the day of Pentecost and addressed thousands with the glorious message of the resurrected Christ. Judas, who also allowed Satan to enter him (Luke 22:3) and take advantage of his weakness, was unable to face his guilt, and went out and committed another wrong. He is not the last servant of God to react in the wrong way toward being overtaken in some sin.

Many, or maybe I should say all of us, have made mistakes and been mistreated by brethren. When I was a young preacher, some of the members where I was working were not doing what I believed they should be doing, and it was very discouraging to me. I was considering moving, but when a beloved brother, James Cope, came to town I dumped my problem on him. Although nearly half a century has passed since that day, his comments to me are still clearly embedded in my mind. He said, in nearly these words: you don't build anything by majoring on the weaknesses. If you major on the weaknesses of your wife, your marriage will soon be on the rocks. If you major on the weaknesses of your business, your business will fail. If you major on the weaknesses in the congregation, you will fail. He said we must major on the good points and minor on the weak points. We should try to build up the weak points, but they should not consume us. When he said that, I realized that two or three people were the ones who were getting all my attention, and over one hundred other people were being completely overlooked! We should realize that some will not be faithful, in the time frame we would prefer, but many are conscientiously trying to grow in Christ. The same is true of our preaching brethren. A few have not taught or lived as they should, but **the vast majority are diligently trying to teach the truth and exemplify it in their lives.** They are not behind closed doors, but their lives are open for the scrutiny of any who wish to observe, and they serve with the realization that "all things are naked and open to the eyes of Him to whom we must give account" (Hebrews 4:13). We have heard that "one rotten apple will spoil the whole barrel," but if we deal properly with the one that is rotten, we will not dispose of the whole barrel! Yes, we are saddened when even one of our preaching brethren is overcome by some evil, but more so, when he allows that failure, like Judas, to destroy his future prospects for serving God. He not only endangers his own soul, but may influence his family and others to follow his destructive ways.

It is my conviction that two classes of preachers should read these good articles. First, those who have made some of the mistakes addressed, and second those who want to avoid making those mistakes. I hope this brief overview will whet your appetite to carefully consider these important lessons and share them with others.

The Preacher's Personal Devotion
Gary Henry

If behind the preacher's door there exists a man who is less devoted to the Lord than the man who presents himself in the pulpit every Sunday, there is a deadly problem. It would be hard to calculate the damage done by such a discrepancy, not only in the preacher's personal life but also in the lives of those whom he influences in his work. The damage may not show up right now, but eventually, a man cannot sow one thing privately and reap something else publicly.

But how can a preacher's personal devotion be lacking? Isn't the fact that he is a preacher evidence that his devotion to the Lord is above average? The honest answer is no. As anyone who has preached very long understands, it is easy for a man's work to become disconnected from the person that he really is, such that he spends his time urging others to devote themselves to the Lord without having any real devotion himself.

Paul wrote about the possibility that a communicator of the gospel might end up being saved even if those whom he taught fell away from the Lord (1 Corinthians 3:15). But he also mentioned the possibility that a man who has saved others by his preaching might end up being lost himself (Philippians 1:15-18).

Too many of us who preach are living double lives. The shocking frequency with which we yield to temptation indicates that the private quality of our faith is less than the public image that we present. And we know that the word for such a double life is *hypocrisy*. To "appear beautiful outwardly" but on the inside to be "full of dead men's bones and all uncleanness" (Matthew 23:27) is an abominable sin.

Isn't it time that we admit the extent of this problem and took steps to resolve it?

The Meaning of "Devotion"

The preacher's personal "devotion" might mean two different things. First, there is what most people would call "devotional time." The preacher has probably urged others to set aside a "quiet time" each day for prayer and Bible study. Does he do this himself? And if he does, is it anything more than a habit or routine?

> The preacher has probably urged others to set aside a "quiet time" each day for prayer and Bible study. Does he do this himself?

But in the larger sense, "devotion" has to do with whether one is devoted to the Lord. It is a bigger question than whether one has a daily devotional time. The word "devotion" is akin to the word "devout," and so the question is one of the preacher's personal devoutness. Having urged others to lead lives that are devout, what about his own devoutness? All of his sermons, Bible classes, home studies, and foreign evangelism aside, how devoted is he to the Lord in the most private part of his own life?

Devotion is much the same as dedication, consecration, sanctification, etc. To be devoted to the Lord is to be reserved for His use alone. And the test of whether we've devoted ourselves to the Lord is not the soundness of our sermon outlines; it's the extent to which we, even in our most private moments, yield ourselves to Him in the obedience of faith. To appear publicly to have yielded ourselves to God is easy; almost anyone can do that. But the test of the preacher's "personal devotion" is what goes on "when no one is looking." If his heart has truly been set apart as the Lord's dwelling place, there will be no conflict between the public and the private man that he is.

Contributing Factors

I suggest that there are at least four factors that have contributed to the "disconnect" between the public profession of preachers and their personal devotion to the Lord.

(1) We allow preaching to degenerate into a "job." Most of us understand that preaching the gospel is more than a "career." We know that we aren't hirelings or time-servers. Even so, the tendency is for us to settle into a routine that, for all practical purposes, makes our work simply a "means of making a living."

With some kinds of secular work, there is little connection between the job and the rest of a man's life. He can leave his "work" at the office or the factory. Since its main purpose is to pay the bills, a "job" need not be connected very closely to the other areas of a man's life.

But gospel preaching is different. It is much more than a means of making a living; it is a way of life. And when it degenerates into a job, the problem is not merely that it demeans the work, but that it disconnects the work from the man. It creates a situation in which a man may go through the motions of doing his "job" without there being any connection between that job and the way he actually lives his life. He can get to the point where he is doing his "work" (and maybe doing it well, as far as others can see) and living a very different life when he is out of the pulpit. When this happens, a man's own spiritual life will rarely be what it ought to be.

(2) We get caught up in the "busyness" of preaching. The work of preaching the gospel is a complex, time-consuming work. And the more a man enjoys the work, the easier it is to over-commit and stay so busy that he has no time for his own spiritual refreshment.

Some preachers pride themselves on the busyness of their schedules, as if the pace of their lives is a badge of honor or an indication of how important they are among the Lord's people. But unrelenting busyness is as good a way to kill one's self spiritually as could be imagined—and it doesn't make any difference that the busyness is *religious* busyness.

Gary Collins once wrote: "Busyness, including busyness with religion and church activities, has been called the 'archenemy of spiritual maturity.' Busy lives have little time for reflection. Never-ending waves of activity keep us from thinking carefully about the important issues in our lives—God, relationships, life purpose, goals, service. Busyness can destroy our relationships. It can stifle spiritual growth and keep us from becoming effective difference makers" (*You Can Make a Difference*, page 49). I agree, and

I believe that busyness, without taking time for personal spiritual growth, is one of the main reasons why those of us who preach often have so little personal devotion to the Lord.

(3) We allow preaching to become a purely intellectual exercise. While the obedience of faith can never be divorced from the doctrinal truths of Christ's Word, there is a danger that we may content ourselves with *nothing more* than those doctrinal truths. Christianity and gospel preaching can come to be just an intellectual exercise in which we weigh arguments for and against certain doctrinal or textual positions. To some extent, all of us are tempted to settle for an academic approach to our work, as if the whole thing were merely a matter of ideas.

> Many preachers never take the next step: preaching lessons that call for changes that they themselves need to make.

Ideas, of course, are the wellspring of our actions, and so they are critically important. But life in Christ involves far more than the intellectual activity of analyzing arguments on disputed points. Based on the truthful doctrines of Christ, there is a *life* to be lived. There is a sense in which the intellectual part of Christianity is the easy part, so it takes real commitment to push beyond the analysis of ideas to the harder challenge of *implementing* those ideas. Unfortunately, however, we often content ourselves with a merely doctrinal approach to Christ and never develop a real devotion to Christ Himself.

Related to this is a tendency for us to spend most of our time analyzing where *other people* are wrong. There was a time when almost every sermon dealt with the errors of those who were "out there" (outside the church building). Eventually, we started preaching sermons that called for changes in the lives of those actually sitting in the pews, and that was a step in the right direction. But many preachers never take the next step: preaching lessons that call for changes that *they themselves* need to make. If our total concentration is on other people's deficiencies, is it any wonder that our own devotion to the Lord becomes deficient?

(4) We are guilty of laziness and a lack of discipline. Here perhaps is the main reason for our lack of personal devotion. For all of our busyness, we've been lazy when it comes to the activities that would have made us strong spiritually. Unwilling to discipline ourselves, we've taken the course of least resistance. And in doing so, we've drifted into personal weakness and vulnerability to sin.

Some Recommendations

If honesty compels us to admit that our devotion to God is lacking, what can we do? Below are some suggestions. This list is not meant to be exhaustive but simply to illustrate the kinds of things we need to pay attention to.

(1) Unceasing self-evaluation. When was the last time you personally took Paul's advice to "examine yourselves as to whether you are in the faith" (2 Corinthians 13:5)? Most of us go for long periods without any serious evaluation of our own faith, and when we do examine ourselves it is rarely with much objectivity or honesty.

Yet we can't grow in our faith without the willingness to be honest about our present position. It takes a person of above-average honesty to admit that his own faith is deficient, especially if he has been preaching for a while, but there is little way to grow spiritually without that kind of frankness.

It would be nice if we could find the key to spiritual strength, lock in the right attitude, and never have to worry about it ever again. But that is not the way life works. Spiritual progress requires *constant adjustments in ourselves*, and these adjustments will not be made unless we see that they *need* to be made. So I recommend that you set up regular times for self-evaluation. Don't let many days go by without checking up on your own spiritual condition.

(2) Accountability to others. Since objectivity and self-honesty are so hard, most of us need *help* in seeing ourselves. Like David who needed Nathan (2 Samuel 12:7-9) and Peter who needed Paul (Galatians 2:11), we need some other trusted person to help us see what we need to see, so that we can make the necessary adjustments.

I recommend that you find some brother who can be a mentor to you or some friend who can meet with you regularly to keep you accountable. As men, we often fail to build relationships with other men that can keep us spiritually honest. As loners and mavericks, we drift away from the Lord (all the while preaching faithful sermons in the pulpit), when a good confidant might have been able to warn us. More openness in our closest relationships—call it "transparency" if you will—is desperately needed.

Specifically, I believe we need to find someone to pray with privately: one or two very close friends in Christ with whom we can pray regularly and honestly. There is nothing quite like praying with a dear brother to motivate us to walk more closely with the Lord.

(3) Keeping God at the center. It should go without saying, but we need to work on keeping God in our minds. It is an amazing thing, but it is possible to expend ourselves completely in the work of God and never really think about Him personally. We become so focused on the "trees" that we lose sight of the "forest," and so busy with the details of the kingdom that we lose touch with the King.

That is one reason a study of the Psalms is so important for us. In the Psalms, we learn a devotion for God Himself, the God who is at the center of all the other truths in the Bible. But whether it is the Psalms or some other part of the Scriptures, we need to be more God-focused in our study—and in our lives.

(4) Daily devotional discipline. No man's faith is going to survive, even if he is a gospel preacher, unless he takes time out from each day to engage in the devotional disciplines of prayer, Bible study, and worship. Whether we do it at the beginning of the day, at the end, or at intervals throughout the day, we simply have to take time for personal growth. Being busy is no excuse for neglecting this discipline. In fact, the busier we are, the *more* we need to take time out.

But mere *Bible study* is not enough. What produces a genuine, vital faith is Bible study *for our own needs*. There is a big difference between studying for a sermon on some subject that someone else needs and studying to fill our own spiritual needs. Many of us have a deficient faith simply because we've never really studied the Bible with any personal purpose.

And when it comes to *prayer*, we need to get beyond the "chit-chat" that characterizes so many of our formal prayers and learn a more honest way of praying. Our faith will begin to grow when we start pouring out our real hearts to God in prayer. If on a given day I don't really want to do what I should, then I need to admit that to the Lord: "Lord, I don't want to. Help me to want to."

> There is a big difference between studying for a sermon on some subject that someone else needs and studying to fill our own spiritual needs.

Along with Bible study and prayer, our daily lives also need to be characterized by *worship*. The worship that we engage in at the church building ought to be the overflow of worship—true praise and adoration of God—that takes places in our most private lives every day of the year.

(5) Practice doing the difficult. As busy as most of us are, it's going to be difficult to do the things that will keep us growing. It wouldn't have been easy for the Lord to stay up all night and pray (Luke 6:12) or to get up before everyone else and pray (Mark 1:35), and it won't be easy for us. Like athletic training, spiritual growth requires doing some difficult things. If we aren't used to doing difficult things, then we're going to have to get "in shape."

"I discipline my body and bring it into subjection," Paul said, "lest, when I have preached to others, I myself should become disqualified" (1 Corinthians 9:27). And to Timothy, he wrote, "Meditate on these things; give yourself entirely to them, that your progress may be evident to all. Take heed to yourself and to the doctrine. Continue in them, for in doing this you will save both yourself and those who hear you" (1 Timothy 4:15, 16).

It is helpful to "practice" the doing of difficult things, just for the "exercise." If it would be difficult for you to get up an hour earlier to pray, I suggest that the very difficulty of the thing might be one good reason to do it. As the weightlifters say, "No pain, no gain." Going to heaven can't be done from a recliner, and spiritual growth is not going to happen in the life of a preacher who avoids difficulty.

So we must become more disciplined in our manner of life. If we don't, there is every reason to believe that we will become, as Paul said, "disqualified."

Conclusion

In short, we must become men of *integrity*. That is, we must be men whose real-world practice is congruent with our Sunday-morning principles, men who consistently walk their talk. Paul urged Timothy to be "an example to the believers in word, in conduct, in love, in spirit, in faith, in purity" (1 Timothy 4:12). Our lives, even in their most private aspects, must *exemplify* the principles that we preach. And truly, there is no greater credibility than that of the man who honestly lives the life that he urges upon others. When others can sense that a man is the "real deal"—when it's obvious that his preaching is simply the overflow of his own private practice—then they will listen with a seriousness that would not otherwise be the case.

So what about you? Are you growing in the faith? When your brethren hear Paul saying, "Meditate on these things; give yourself entirely to them, that your *progress* may be evident to all" (1 Timothy 4:15), do they think of you as a man who is making progress in your own spiritual life?

And what about me? Is my faith genuine? Am I really the person I present myself as being when I'm in the pulpit? And when I preach, am I merely presenting *facts* that I've gleaned from books or am I recommending a *life* that I myself am living? If it is not the latter, then I should be gravely concerned and prepare myself either to repent or quit preaching.

As preachers, the impact that we have on others is greatly affected by the genuineness of our own godly fear. If we find that our preaching has little impact, we need to ponder the words of God to those of shallow faith in Ezekiel's day: "'And I will sanctify My great name, which has been profaned among the nations, which you have profaned in their midst; and the nations shall know that I am the LORD,' says the Lord GOD, 'when I am hallowed in you before their eyes'" (Ezekiel 36:23).

There is no greater dishonor to God than for His own people to disrespect Him, and there is no greater disrespect than that of the preacher whose personal devotion is merely pretended. May we who preach—*every single one of us*—do whatever it takes, before it's too late, to deepen our reverence and enrich our walk with the Lord.

The Preacher's Daily Discipline
Mark Roberts

In a breakthrough study begun in the 1960s at Stanford University the single trait absolutely essential for success in all areas of life was isolated and identified. Professor Walter Mischel discovered this secret in an experiment he did with children. Mischel took a four-year-old child, sat him down at a table, and put one delicious marshmallow directly in front of him. The child was told that he could eat the marshmallow at any time. However, if the child would simply wait and not eat the marshmallow for fifteen or twenty minutes he would be rewarded with a second marshmallow. The choice was simple: one marshmallow now, or two marshmallows later. The researcher then left the room.

Of course, many children ate the one marshmallow only seconds after the researcher left. About one-third of the subjects were "grabbers" and went for immediate gratification. Another one-third waited a little while but then caved in and ate the one marshmallow. However, about one-third of the kids waited. They successfully fought the urge to enjoy one marshmallow now so they could have that second marshmallow later. They showed self-discipline.

The research team then tracked all the children as they grew up and made their way through life. Not surprisingly, the kids who demonstrated self-control were more successful in every phase of life. They did better in school, scored an average of 210 points higher on their SATs, got better jobs, and even enjoyed better marriages. Self-discipline was, as shown in Mischel's study, the key to success in every area of life. [1]

---

[1] This study is cited in numerous papers and articles. For an excellent summation see Kerry Patterson's book *Influencer*, McGraw-Hill, New York, 2008, page 115ff.

Although Mischel's study did not reveal if any of those children grew up to be Gospel preachers, this writer would argue that self-discipline is also the key to being a successful preacher. Why? First, self-discipline is one of the essentials for successful Christianity. Christians are told to "add to their knowledge *self-control*"(2 Peter 1:6; see also 2 Corinthians 4:17-18). Jesus tells us that daily self-discipline is at the very heart of genuine discipleship (Luke 9:23). If one cannot control himself, he will always be a mediocre Christian. Bluntly put, mediocre Christians make mediocre preachers. Secondly, the unique temptations, problems, and dilemmas faced by preachers require large amounts of self-discipline. Indeed, all of the sins dealt with in this book must be defeated, at some point, with the will power to say "No" to what is wrong and "Yes" to what is right. However, beyond just those temptations, the day-to-day life of a preacher demands significant self-control. Being an effective preacher—spending time in study and prayer, working closely with an eldership, dealing with difficult situations in a local church, helping people caught in sin's tangled web, enduring criticism and much more—requires discipline. In short, much of the preacher's life depends on rejecting one marshmallow now in favor of a second marshmallow later. This chapter sets the stage for much of the rest of this book by exploring the preacher's daily disciplines. As we do that, we will not be focusing on specific sins or temptations but instead want to develop the positive value of being self-controlled and self-disciplined every day in the work of a Gospel preacher.

> If one cannot control himself, he will always be a mediocre Christian. Mediocre Christians make mediocre preachers.

That begins with the discipline of planning the work. It is not a sin to forget a Bible study appointment, or to have to print the bulletin late on Saturday night, but those problems may be a comment on one's self-discipline. The trouble here centers on the difference in the preacher's job and "regular" jobs. In most workplaces there is a boss who sets the daily agenda or a time clock that measures hours spent on the job, or both. Yet preachers usually have neither. The preacher's work-day is often completely unmonitored. Many churches do not even care if a preacher keeps regular office hours. As long as the preacher is ready to teach his Bible classes and has two sermons prepared on Sunday (and handles a few other duties) the brethren are content to let him schedule his time as he wishes. That represents a challenge to the preacher's personal discipline because he has to decide what to do and when to do it.

> If a preacher cannot discipline himself to work hard, in the office and at his studies his life will quickly become miserable.

So the preacher steps into his office on Monday morning and the week looms large before him, full of promise and opportunity. There seems to be plenty of time for everything, so why not surf the Internet for a moment? Then some emails need to be replied to, and of course, since someone emailed a joke some time is spent finding an equally humorous funny to send back. Checking Facebook takes only a minute, a minute that quickly stretches to fifteen minutes or more. Then a quick game of Freecell (or two) and before one knows it, half the day is spent. After lunch the preacher has an appointment to fish or hunt or golf … and a day is now gone. A modern day updating of an old proverb speaks to this: "A little checking of the email, a little twittering, a little folding of the hands around the mouse and poverty will come upon you like a robber, and want like an armed man." The trouble is a lack of self-control and daily self-discipline.

If a preacher cannot discipline himself to work, and work hard, in the office and at his studies, his life will quickly become miserable. A failure to plan out and complete his assigned responsibilities will mean he ends up neglecting his family as he puts in long hours in the evenings to make up for wasted time during the day. Making matters worse, his preaching will be poor on Sunday because he was frantically throwing together something Saturday night (or downloading someone else's sermon off the Internet) and his lack of preparation will be apparent to all. That means the brethren are unhappy with him, and the church stagnates and feels discontented. The unproductive preacher may want to blame others for the problems at hand, but he knows where the real trouble lies, and that he is cheating his brethren out of honest work for an honest wage.

Every preacher should have a plan for his work, and then must work that plan. Part of that work is self-improvement. Preachers should ask themselves "What am I doing to better myself? What books can I read to grow and develop and be more effective? What am I reading and studying apart from what I must prepare to teach in Bible class or from the pulpit?" Preachers need to develop themselves so as to be continuously growing and fresh. There are no continuing education requirements in preaching, but perhaps there should be! Preachers who are not reading, studying, writing, and thinking will grow stale and their work with a congregation will reflect that. The wise preacher selects books that sharpen him, maintains a strict regimen of daily Bible reading and prayer, and even works regularly on longtime projects (like writing class material for future use or articles for the church's website). Ecclesiastes 10:10 extols the value of sharpening the saw: "If the iron is blunt, and one does not sharpen the edge, he must use more strength, but wisdom helps one to succeed." It takes self-discipline to resist the urge to check email one more time, or play another game of Mafia Wars on Facebook or sleep in or while away the hours with Fox News and television. Yet constant and steady work on self bears tremendous rewards for the disciplined preacher. The planning that makes that happen can only occur when we have enough discipline to stop what appears to be so urgent (or enjoyable) in this moment and wait for that second marshmallow.

There is more to preaching than just personal study and growth, however. There are sermons to write and visits to make and classes to teach. This means a preacher needs self-discipline with *time management.* A preacher's life is filled with all sorts of responsibilities and appointments. Church members ask him to do all sorts of activities – everything from looking up a needed passage, to visiting a neighbor, to setting up a Bible study. Along with those tasks are the never-changing obligations of sermon and Bible class preparation, deadlines that must be met every Sunday and Wednesday. That all must be meshed with an ever-changing calendar of elders meetings, trips to the hospital and funeral home, home Bible studies, and family obligations. It is a dizzying whirlwind to keep up with! The disciplined preacher will want some sort of systematic method to track all of these varying responsibilities, obligations, and engagements. He does this because he knows the value of time. Paul admonishes "Look carefully then how you walk, not as unwise but as wise, *making the best use of the time*, because the days are evil" (Ephesians 5:15-16).

For many preachers, the way to maximize time and be self-disciplined with it means some sort of planner or organizer. Today there are many choices readily available, everything from carefully structured commercially available systems to simple calendars and task lists on your cell phone. Some preachers rely on nothing more than a stack of three-by-five index cards in their pocket or a small wire bound notebook. What one uses does not matter nearly as much as having something that works well and is used consistently. A planner provides a place for everything to come together and be kept together. Post-it notes and scraps of paper with scribbles on them stashed and stuck all over everywhere make it easy to miss engagements and forget assignments. Keep it all in one place, and it is much easier to keep life all together. The planner is that place. Further, a planner provides accountability. Am I doing what I said I would today? What am I supposed to be doing today anyway? Part of daily discipline is managing time and managing it well.

A final key part of *daily discipline* that must not be neglected is the discipline required to maintain the physical body. Paul tells us that bodily exercise is not as profitable as godliness, but he does admit that bodily exercise is of "some value" (1 Timothy 4:8). Let us focus on the "little bit" gained by caring for the body. Preaching can be demanding, rigorous, and physically exhausting. What a shame for capable men to be lost in the Kingdom's cause with heart attacks, strokes, and other physical illnesses simply because they did not eat right and exercise! Does it make sense to carefully maintain an automobile, changing its oil and having preventive maintenance done regularly, and then fail to take the same care with a far more valuable "machine," our body? Even worse, some preachers are dangerously obese, a condition that announces to everyone they are not disciplined in their own eating habits. How effective can such a man be in teaching others about self-discipline when it is so obvious he does not practice what he preaches? Even worse, what of those who "burn out" in preaching because their bodies were not in condition to keep up with the pace their work required? Sometimes preachers over-promise and over-tax themselves, trying to do too much. Sometimes preachers could do more, however, if they simply would take a little better care of themselves. Further, it is worth noting that fatigue can be a contributing factor in depression and cynicism and poor decision making. How many preachers who have fallen into scandalous sin were exhausted and stressed? It seems that temptation and sin always find the over-worked, over-stressed, over-tired man. This all means that while preachers do not need to be fitness nuts they need to be disciplined enough to keep themselves in "good operating condition" so they can serve the Master.

These areas of life and work show the need for self-discipline. But what good does it do to know self-control's value and importance if we then do not do all we can to acquire it? Here are five ideas that help build self-control.

> . But what good does it do to know self-control's value and importance if we then do not do all we can to acquire it

First, one must believe self-control can be developed. We must reject our culture's lie that self-control is somehow related to genetics or inherited from others. Many seem content to say "I am just not very self-disciplined" as if this is not their fault and nothing can be done about it. Professor Mischel proved otherwise. He followed up his first marshmallow study with another study in which he placed children who had demonstrated poor self-control with adults who modeled self-discipline skills. Quickly the subjects who had previously failed to control self and wait for the second marshmallow did what they saw the adults doing, and controlled themselves. Mischel concluded that self-control can be taught and can be learned. This only makes sense. The Bible would not call for us to be self-disciplined if this is an inborn trait no one can develop! If we are telling ourselves that we cannot improve then we are beat before we start and out of line with the Scriptures' teaching. We can develop self-control.

Secondly, set small goals. Saying "I want to be more self-controlled" is such a large and vaguely defined goal that it does not help much. Everybody already wants to be more self-controlled. Wanting to improve does not cause change. Self-discipline is grown when we identify specific areas of life where we need more self-control and carefully monitor our activity in that part of life. So, saying "I want to complete my daily Bible reading every day before I check email or do anything else" is a much better goal. It is clear and definable. It can be easily checked, and progress can even be recorded and charted. Being faithful in small things leads to the ability to be faithful in larger things (note Matthew 25:21). Constant progress, even as we take small steps, helps build a sense of mastery and increasing self-discipline.

Thirdly, prepare for defeat and be ready to begin again. It is impossible to go from no self-control to fully self-controlled over night. There will be small successes followed by a return to old habits and failure. If we give up the first time we fail we will never grow in self-discipline. The Bible clearly understands the need for beginning again. 1 John 2:1 tells us "My little children, I am writing these things to you so that you may not sin. But if anyone does sin, we have an advocate with the Father, Jesus Christ the righteous." Surely this is not an excuse for sin but it is strong encouragement to not let failure be fatal, but instead to start over and try again. In the battle to grow self-control it may take many "new beginnings" to become as disciplined as we would like.

Fourth, learn from past mistakes. Paul readily acknowledged his past sin and had obviously learned many lessons from them, such as humility (1 Timothy 1:15). Yet all that some seem to learn from their mistakes is how to blame others! Preachers who are serious about developing self-discipline will carefully examine themselves when they fail to wait for that second marshmallow. They will ask, "What happened? Why couldn't I be more disciplined? How could this have been prevented? Is there a pattern to my failures?" Thinking through failure in the past leads to being better prepared to meet that problem in the future.

Finally, and perhaps most important, plan for what to do when one's self-control is challenged. Joseph's classic story contains this significant note: "And as she spoke to Joseph day after day, *he would not listen to her, to lie beside her or to be with her*" (Genesis 39:10). Joseph's self-control was severely tested by Potiphar's wife and her sexual advances. What did Joseph do about it? He made plans to help himself by avoiding her entirely! Yet too many never think this far in advance, and so are trapped in sin or in self-defeating bad habits. Does a certain TV channel always seem to be showing something that appeals to the lust of the flesh, and when one is flipping channels somehow the TV always ends up there for a little too long? Block that channel! If one is struggling with diet and over eating, empty the pantry of cookies, chips and candies. If Brother Sharp Tongue's criticisms of one's preaching causes anger, plan ahead exactly what to say, perhaps even write out a script, so that one is prepared to be under control and disciplined even in that stressful moment. When we are tempted to do wrong and we really want to enjoy sin instead of doing what is right, what is our plan to do right anyway? The answer to that question is often the very point that separates failure from success, losing control from being self-disciplined. It is planning ahead and thinking through difficult situations that takes self-control to another level. Even if our plans do not work, they give us something to learn, review and work on. Proverbs 22:3 says, "The prudent sees danger and hides himself, but the simple go on and suffer for it." The self-disciplined preacher plans his hiding place!

> "A man without self-control is like a city broken into and left without walls"

Hopefully if we go behind the preacher's door we will not find the preacher gazing at a single marshmallow trying to resist the urge to immediately gobble it down. Yet what we will find behind every preacher's door, and as part of every preacher's life, is the ongoing battle with self and the need for self-discipline. Solomon says, "A man without self-control is like a city broken into and left without walls" (Proverbs 25:28). Too many preachers' lives have been broken and wrecked because they lacked self-control. Let us see the great need for daily discipline and learn how to develop it so that we can be strong and capable men, ready to serve our Lord.

The Preacher's Ethics
Matthew Allen

It has certainly been an honor for me to preach the gospel of Christ. The influence of godly and spiritual brothers and sisters has had a significant impact on my wife, my children, and me. We have been blessed with some of the most precious and warm relationships with brethren across the globe. I feel that God has used my life decision to preach as an opportunity to strengthen me into the person I am now. I am a better person because I preach.

> **Those who refuse to live up to the high standard that comes along with preaching should find another profession.**

The work of preaching brings forth incredible responsibilities. Perhaps the most important aspect of the effectiveness of any preacher is his influence and example. If brethren have the perception that there are significant shortcomings with a preacher's personal life, then it will be extremely difficult for his preaching and teaching to have traction. This is why Paul exhorted Timothy to, *let no one look down upon your youthfulness, but rather in speech, conduct, love, faith, and purity, show yourself an example of those who believe,* 1 Timothy 4:12. Any Christian, who preaches or not, should regularly examine himself to make sure what he/she professes matches up with the conduct by which he/she lives. For the preacher, this is especially important. Jimmy Jividen (2007) writes, "He must seek to live up to the ideal he tells others to follow... the effectiveness of his message is hindered or enhanced by the life he lives" (12-13). Those who refuse to live up to the high standard that comes along with preaching should find another profession. Timothy was expected to *pay close attention* to himself and his teaching over the long term, 1 Timothy 4:16. This involves personal discipline and a steadfast commitment to the principles found within the word of God.

Equally important to the necessity of a consistent and positive example, is the need for a preacher to approach his work with honesty and transparency. Christians are to *have regard for what is honorable, not only in the sight of the Lord, but also in the sight of men,* 2 Corinthians 8:21. We are to lead lives of dignity and honor. These qualities are achieved by a commitment to good communication with congregational leadership, the congregation itself and a sincere faith in God.

Good communication is a dual responsibility. Congregational leadership should communicate frequently with the preacher. An eldership has the responsibility to help bear some of the load of the preacher and build a relationship on trust. But, equally important is the minister's responsibility to engage in regular dialogue with the eldership. Because of poor attitudes, communication with an eldership and/or the congregation can sometimes find itself in peril. How many gospel preachers exhibit a "me vs. them" mentality? Carl McMurray once wrote, "Though a few (elders) may be worthy of it, usually they are not paid for their hours, their visits, or their grief as the preacher is." Elders should be held in high esteem and be respected by the preacher. *Appreciate those who diligently labor among you, and have charge over you in the Lord and give you instruction,* 1 Thessalonians 5:12-13. These thoughts of Paul should govern the attitude of the located preacher. Preachers are not above instruction and guidance. While the perspectives of preachers and elders can vary greatly, a preacher must never forget that when he operates in a located work, he places himself under the oversight and authority of the elders. They, not he, are over the flock, Acts 20:28. Hebrews 13:17 exhorts Christians to *obey your leaders and submit to them, for they keep watch over your soul as those who will give an account. Let them do this with joy and not with grief...* The biblical view of submission means that one arranges himself under another person. While the gospel preacher may not always agree with the eldership's judgment or reasoning, he is responsible to heed their advice and guidance. This is submission. When preaching on the eldership and the congregation's role in working with them, we often speak on these matters with authority and think in terms of the congregation following through on God's expectations. Are there some preachers who act as if these expectations are not applicable to them? Just as each individual member has the responsibility to be in submission, so does the preacher. If our viewpoint and perspective of the eldership becomes jaded, it can easily lead to a breakdown in honesty and transparency in the work of a preacher. One can find himself inside a situation where he is not inclined to disclose certain things about his work. Even though things may seem insignificant, it is far better to be out in the open on matters associated with our work, than to give off the perception that something is being hidden or held back.

What about the located preacher who works inside a congregation that does not have an eldership? Honesty, openness, and good communication are just as essential. When moving to a congregation, the preacher and the congregation most always have a verbal agreement (sometimes it is a written agreement) as to expectations on salary, time off, and in what ways the work will be conducted. No matter how men may act inside a men's business meeting or how relationships may change as time goes on, the preacher always has the responsibility to honor his part of the agreement with the congregation. Just because others act in an ungodly fashion, does not give the preacher an excuse. The same "me vs. them" attitude that can exist between a preacher and elders can reside inside the preacher who works with a congregation with no eldership. This perspective must be avoided at all costs.

Honesty and ethical behavior carries over into the everyday work of the gospel preacher. For example, how faithful are we in responding to and following through on instructions handed down by an eldership? Is our dedication to the completion of the task and faithful submission to their wishes clearly seen? Is our good character and reputation enhanced by our punctuality and promptness at meetings, Bible studies, and other engagements? Can brethren see our willingness to cooperate with others inside the congregation? The same principles we preach on the employee/employer relationship are applicable to the servant of God who preaches. We are to *serve with sincerity of heart, fearing the Lord. Whatever you do, do your work heartily, as for the Lord, rather than for men, knowing that from the Lord you will receive the reward of the inheritance. It is the Lord Christ whom you serve,* Colossians 3:22b-24. Too many gospel preachers are not good stewards of their time and essentially rob the congregation they labor with when they slack off with their work to invest in their personal hobbies and pet projects. Over time, this approach to the work of preaching will reap negative dividends. Remember, the congregation reasonably expects a preacher to give a fair amount of his time to teaching and to the preparation for teaching. While a preacher's work is "open ended", he must be careful not to abuse the trust, which has been given to him (Warden, 2007).

We must also openly communicate with the congregation concerning the time we will be away from our located work for gospel meetings, attendance at lectureships, and personal time. There can be a strong temptation to hold back in this aspect of communication. Everyone who has preached for some time has endured the ribbing of brethren who might say something like, "You only work one day of the week," "You are always gone for gospel meetings," and "You really think you need a vacation?" While most people are simply joking, we can guard against a negative perception forming when we invest ourselves in our work and people can see the fruit of our labor. I believe this perception can be held back by an eldership that is proactive with brethren in explaining the day-to-day rigors of preaching to brethren. Preachers can be subject to burnout and suffer physical and mental strain. Even if there are actions being taken to curb a negative perception, a preacher can still yield to the temptation to hold back on communication about time off. We tell ourselves that it would be easier to say nothing at all than put up with the jesting and scrutiny of brethren. We tell ourselves that brethren simply do not understand what it is like to be a preacher. They do not have to endure the sleepless nights, 24/7/365 telephone calls, and the constant pressure of being there for others. It is true that most persons inside a congregation do not understand all that a preacher's work can encompass. Not all of a preacher's work is inside the office, behind a desk. Some do not get it, and unfortunately, they most likely will not get it. This fact, however, should not cause us to believe that we can justify our calling the shots without seeking permission or passing along information, etc.

How well do we do in honoring the agreement we made on the number of gospel meetings we schedule each year? Do we stick to the allotted number of vacation days to be off? Are there clear expectations on how many days of the week will be taken off? Have arrangements been made for "comp time" if a preacher finds himself working on his scheduled days off? A preacher who is proactive will take measures in advance to head off any potential problems. Most likely, we know some preachers who are quick to ignore the elders and/or congregational expectations on the number of meetings they preach. They have the idea that they somehow deserve it, or that brethren simply will not care. The brethren in the local church family may not care, but honesty demands that communication be made in advance of a meeting or time off being scheduled. Generally, an eldership will look down on a preacher when it perceives or realizes that he makes plans and then demands permission at a later time. Perhaps this kind of behavior may not matter too much initially, but at a later time, now looking through a more negative lens, elders/brethren may remember their displeasure and use this against the preacher in making a decision on whether or not to retain his services.

If we find self succumbing to the temptation to be less than transparent and conceal some action or situation in life it will come out in time.

The bottom line is that we need to be honest with self and honest with those for whom we serve. In the Sermon on the Mount, Jesus taught, *let your statement be, "yes, yes" or "no, no" anything beyond these is of evil,* (Matthew 5:37). We must honor the commitment we made when moving to a local work. If circumstances and needs have changed, then it may be time to arrange a meeting with the leadership and seek changes in the agreement you have with a congregation. Many elderships have policies in place that the longer a preacher remains with a congregation the more time off he is allowed. This is done to encourage longevity in working with a congregation and should be viewed as a reward for years of faithful work and dedication to a local church. I believe most elderships (and congregations) want to be fair to their preacher and have a respect for him and his work. Their respect will continue to grow as they see a preacher's dedication to maintaining his example and his commitment to living by example and faithfulness. Generally, elderships want to keep the preacher happy, but remember their first responsibility is not to the preacher's overall pleasure and comfort. Their first responsibility is to the congregation that they oversee and to what is best for it. Remember, the eldership has voluntarily placed themselves in a position to serve and they will give an account for their actions, (Hebrews 13:17b).

Know this. If we find self succumbing to the temptation to be less than transparent and conceal some action or situation in life it will come out in time. When we deceive self into thinking that hiding a mistake or unfortunate set of circumstances is alright, the result can be devastating. Maybe there has been a personal shortcoming, or an issue inside of the preacher's family. Would it not be better for congregational leadership to find out directly from you, rather than chasing down a rumor or receiving the information in some other indirect manner? Jesus said, *But there is nothing covered up that will not be revealed, and hidden that will not be known. Accordingly, what you have said in the dark will be heard in the light, and what you have whispered in the inner rooms will be proclaimed upon the housetops,* Luke 12:1-3. Breakdowns of this nature can and will result in a lack of trust. This trust is vital to a preacher's work. As gospel preachers, we should never give an eldership a reason to doubt. Terry Jones (2009) has written, "Preachers can never work effectively without enjoying confidence from the elders. When this trust ceases to exist, it is time for that congregation to seek another preacher."

There is a virtue that, when made a central part of the preacher's life, will help diminish the problem of poor communication and an improper perspective of the eldership. When this virtue is applied, a commitment to the highest of ethical standards will be applied. Those who place this character trait into their daily routine will lead a life of complete and total dependence upon Jesus Christ. What is the virtue we need? Humility. The simple fact is that many gospel preachers need a good dose of humility. Paul wrote, *(do) not think more highly of (yourself) that (you) ought to think, but think so as to have sound judgment,* (Romans 12:3). God has given our talents, abilities, opportunities, and work as a gospel preacher to us. We are not self-made. We are who we are because God and good people (friends and family) have helped us along the way. The humble heart will be willing to lay his fears and concerns down at the feet of God and depend upon Him in complete and total trust. Even if a preacher finds himself in an unfair situation, God will still be there, every step of the way. The Holy Spirit said, *God is opposed to the proud, but gives grace to the humble,* (James 4:6.)

When the gospel preacher dedicates himself to the simple principles of honesty, transparency, and humility, he will find himself at peace. He will find a healthy relationship with his elders and the congregation. Both the preacher and the elders can look at one another with a warm and genuine respect and admiration. He will be blessed with the strong and close bonds with brethren of like precious faith. And, finally, because of his faithfulness to his commitment he will be able to work with confidence trusting (knowing) that his diligent service will be met with approval from the Lord.

Bibliography

Jividen, J. (2007, September), Leading by Example: The Personal Life of a Preacher. *Gospel Advocate, CXLIX (9) pp.12-13.*

Jones, T.G. (2009), *Maintaining a Good Elder/Preacher Relationship.* Retired Dec. 1, 2009 from Carolina Messenger: www.carolinamessenger.com/images/079505.pdf

McMurray, C. (2003, October). Preaching Training. (D.L. Henderson, Ed.) *Straitway.*

Warden, D. (2007, September). Principle and Relationships: Maintaining a Balance. *Gospel Advocate, CXLIX (9),* p.20.

The Preacher's Battle with Pornography
Jason Hardin

I'm not going to expound on Matthew 5:27-30. You already know what that passage says. I'm not going to recount Joseph's story of courageous integrity from Genesis 39. You've preached from that text yourself. I'm not going to list the dozens of clear and concise proverbs that warn about the dangers of sexual immorality. You could quote most of them anyway.

As a part of the target audience of this book, you already know. You are painfully aware of the fact that your personal battle with pornography doesn't hinge solely on the knowledge in your head. As a preacher, you're familiar with the biblical facts. You've quoted the statistics. You've conveyed to your brethren the confessions of penitent prisoners of the war against sexual immorality. You've seen the tears of heartbroken spouses. You've preached repeatedly about the necessity to "cast off the works of darkness and put on the armor of light" (Romans 13:12). You know.

And yet, the battle for purity of heart rages on in your life. Sometimes you win. Too often, however, you lose. You understand all too well the vivid, personal grief described by Paul in Romans 7:14-24.

For we know that the law is spiritual, but I am of the flesh, sold under sin. For I do not understand my own actions. For I do not do what I want, but I do the very thing I hate. Now if I do what I do not want, I agree with the law, that it is good. So now it is no longer I who do it, but sin that dwells within me. For I know that nothing good dwells in me, that is, in my flesh. For I have the desire to do what is right, but not the ability to carry it out. For I do not do the good I want, but the evil I do not want is what I keep on doing. Now if I do what I do not want, it is no longer I who do it, but sin that dwells within me.

So I find it to be a law that when I want to do right, evil lies close at hand.

For I delight in the law of God, in my inner being, but I see in my members another law waging war against the law of my mind and making me captive to the law of sin that dwells in my members. Wretched man that I am! Who will deliver me from this body of death?

> **Wisdom encourages us to stand at the trailhead of this dark, forbidden pathway and think before we take another step - at what cost will this fleeting pleasure come?**

Paul's problem didn't stem from a lack of knowledge, or a disagreement with the law, or even a lack of desire to do what was right. Paul's problem was that sin had taken up residence within. His inner being delighted in the law of God, but his flesh was waging war—war against what he intellectually knew. And at some point, Paul had turned the throne of his soul over to sin. When sin is allowed to reign in a mortal body, it makes you obey its passions (Romans 6:12). When you present your members to sin as instruments for unrighteousness, sin has dominion over you (Romans 6:14). When you surrender yourself as an obedient slave of sin, it will lead you all the way to death (Romans 6:16, 23). Paul had been there. I have been there. So have you.

Counting the Cost

One of the most sobering things a man can do is to count the cost of being defeated on this front of the war for his soul. It's certainly a biblical principle. In the context of warnings against sexual immorality, Solomon asks in Proverbs 6:27-28, "Can a man carry fire next to his chest and his clothes not be burned? Or can one walk on hot coals and his feet not be scorched?" Wisdom encourages us to stand at the trailhead of this dark, forbidden pathway and think before we take another step—at what cost will this fleeting pleasure come? Begin walking this trail, and elements of your life will be unalterably burned. Decide to follow this path, and some of the most precious aspects of your existence will be forever scorched.

As I look down this pathway and count the possible cost, the price is steep. Fail to stand steadfast on the sexual immorality front of the war for my soul, and the collateral damage could be devastating.

- I will have turned my back on the only sacrifice suitable to atone for my sins.
- I will have reopened the door to a fearful expectation of judgment..
- I will have spurned the very Son of God.
- I will have profaned the blood of the covenant by which I was sanctified.
- I will have outraged the Spirit of grace.
- I will have declared myself an enemy of the Almighty.
- I will have exchanged the pure holiness of my heavenly Father for the fleeting and foolish passions of my former ignorance.
- I will have compromised my new identity in Christ.
- I will have become a prisoner of war to sin and corruption.
- I will have destroyed countless dreams for the future as a preacher and author.
- I will have shattered elements of my influence with others that has taken years to build.
- I will have made a mockery of the love Christ expects of me as a husband.
- I will have demolished years of trust with my wife that might never be rebuilt.
- I will have caused indescribable pain and embarrassment to my best friend.
- I will have threatened the dynamics of sexual intimacy for the rest of my marriage.
- I will have emotionally scarred my daughters beyond comprehension. The impact my sexual sins could have on their own sexuality, self-esteem, and their view of men is immeasurable.
- I will have endangered healthy relationships with my sisters in Christ in countless ways.
- I will be forced to acknowledge that I foolishly learned nothing from the examples of those who have fallen in the same ways before me.
- I will have shamed my physical family.
- I will have shamed my spiritual family.
- I will almost certainly have forfeited my opportunity to preach where I am currently located and might never enjoy another opportunity again.
- I will have severely disappointed and hurt those I have helped lead to Christ.
- I will have undermined every good thing I ever did in the minds of many.
- I will have brought great satisfaction to the adversary of my soul.
- I will have dishonored the glory of God, which I was created and redeemed to reflect.

The more I add to the list, the longer the list becomes. I would encourage you to make a similar, very personal list. Do so, and the wisdom of Proverbs 7:21-23 will become frighteningly real. "With much seductive speech she persuades him; with her smooth talk she compels him. All at once he follows her, as an ox goes to the slaughter, or as a stag is caught fast till an arrow pierces its liver; as a bird rushes into a snare; he does not know that it will cost him his life."

David's transgressions were serious symptoms of the greatest ailment of all - not treasuring God above every other person, pleasure, and thing.

God's Steadfast Love Is Better Than Life

And so why do we sin? Having counted the cost, why would we choose to do what we know to be wrong? Why would we be willing to gamble so much for so little?

Simply put, we prefer other things, other people, and other pleasures more than we prefer God. And that is precisely why something as addictive as pornography is so difficult to defeat. We can readily identify the shortcomings, we can easily pinpoint the bad habits, we can drill encouraging slogans into our heads, we can establish a variety of accountability safeguards…and continue to be sifted as wheat! How? Why? We have failed to accurately diagnose the root of the problem.

Pornography is a problem, but it is not **THE** problem. Pornography is a sinful symptom of the problem. Sexual self-gratification is a problem, but it is not **THE** problem. Self-gratification is an ugly manifestation of the problem. The adulterous affair is certainly a problem, but it is not **THE** problem. The adulterous affair is a wicked reflection of the problem. **THE** problem is preferring other things, other people, and other pleasures more than we prefer God.

Isn't it interesting what *isn't* in Psalm 51? David had committed adultery, lied, manipulated, and murdered. And yet, in his classic psalm of confession, not one of those sins is specifically identified. Neither Bathsheba nor Uriah are named. Why is that? **Because David's transgressions were serious symptoms of the greatest ailment of all—not**

treasuring God above every other person, pleasure, and thing.

"I know my transgressions, and my sin is ever before me. Against you, you only, have I sinned and done what is evil in your sight....Create in me a clean heart, O God, and renew a right spirit within me. Cast me not away from your presence, and take not your Holy Spirit from me. Restore to me the joy of your salvation, and uphold me with a willing spirit" (Psalm 51:3-4, 10-12).

Like Paul after him, David's sin did not stem from ignorance. David's shortcoming was not the result of a long-held, deep-seeded disagreement with the laws of God. He was a man after God's own heart! But on that night, **David wanted illicit sexual gratification more than he wanted God.** In the months ahead, David treasured his sinful secret more than he treasured God. When the situation grew desperate, David feared the awful truth being revealed more than he feared God. When backed into a corner, David demonstrated more of a willingness to shed innocent blood than to honestly and penitently cast himself before the feet of the God who already knew what David had done. David was exactly right when he confessed, "I have sinned against the LORD" (2 Samuel 12:13).

The same is true for us. "The body is not meant for sexual immorality, but for the Lord, and the Lord for the body" (1 Corinthians 6:13). "Put on the Lord Jesus Christ, and make no provision for the flesh, to gratify its desires" (Romans 13:14). "God has not called us for impurity, but in holiness. Therefore whoever disregards this, disregards not man but God, who gives his Holy Spirit to you" (1 Thessalonians 4:7-8).

Every day we are faced with decisions, opportunities, tests, and trials. We know what God has said, but will we supplement our knowledge with integrity? We know what God expects, but will we fortify biblical truth with personal character? We will preach about righteousness, self-control and the coming judgment on Sunday, but will we reinforce the facts with faith on Monday?

Are the blessings that flow from your connection with God more gratifying than the sinful images that can flow through your connection to the Internet? If not, you will find yourself enslaved to pornography. Late at night, when everyone else is in bed, is the urge to pray stronger than the tugs of sin on the garment of your flesh? If not, sin will seize an opportunity to deceive you. "Blessed are the pure in heart, for they shall see God" (Matthew 5:8). Does the blessed assurance of seeing God mean more to you in the moment than illicit self-gratification? If not, you will continue to do the very thing you hate.

> ## Until you treasure God as more precious than pornography, you will continue to be in bondage to pornography.

Until you treasure God as more precious than pornography, you will continue to be in bondage to pornography. Until you cherish God as more satisfying than all illicit pleasures, you will continue to be enslaved to the lusts of your flesh. Until the pain of being separated from God is greater than the pain of repentance, you won't give up your sin.

And so God invites you to personally accept the challenge of Psalm 34:8. "Oh taste and see that the LORD is good! Blessed is the man who takes refuge in him!" God is to be delighted in and savored, not just intellectually known and used in whatever ways we see fit.

How refreshing and liberating are the words of David in Psalm 63:1-3! "O God, you are my God; earnestly I seek you; my soul thirsts for you; my flesh faints for you, as in a dry and weary land where there is no water. So I have looked upon you in the sanctuary, beholding your power and glory. Because your steadfast love is better than life, my lips will praise you."

An intimate relationship with God is better than the highest sexual high. Purposeful communion with him is more enjoyable than any earthly gratification. A consistent walk with him is more thrilling than any fleeting deviance. His refining fellowship is more exhilarating than anything this world will ever offer. Forsake the mirages and flee to him!

Temptations will come, but let them come. God is more powerful. God is more satisfying. "No temptation has overtaken you that is not common to man. God is faithful, and he will not let you be tempted beyond your ability, but with the temptation he will also provide the way of escape, that you may be able to endure it" (1 Corinthians 10:13).

You Must Wage War

"I see in my members another law waging war against the law of my mind" (Romans 7:23). "Your passions are at war within you" (James 4:1). "Abstain from the passions of the flesh, which wage war against your soul" (1 Peter 2:11). War is upon and around and within you, whether you acknowledge it or not. The good news is, "There is therefore now no condemnation for those who are in Christ Jesus....We are more than conquerors through him who loved us" (Romans 8:1, 37). But if you would stand and remain on the side of ultimate victory, you must make a wholehearted declaration of all-out, relentless, holy war against your sin. Enough compromise. Make war! No more procrastination. Make war! Refuse the rationalizations. Make war!

Be vigilant. "Keep your heart with all vigilance, for from it flow the springs of life" (Proverbs 4:23). "Be sober-minded; be watchful. Your adversary the devil prowls around like a roaring lion, seeking someone to devour" (1 Peter 5:8). Begin your day with prayer. Saturate your day with prayer. End your day with prayer. "Lead me not into temptation, but deliver me from evil."

Be a person of radical integrity. Make up your mind right now. Dare to stand like Joshua, having chosen in advance whom you will serve (Joshua 24:15). Unashamedly pledge your allegiance before another temptation hits.

Fight for the joy of your salvation. Hunger and thirst for those superior pleasures that can sever the roots of the lies of this world. Take honest inventory. What enhances your joy in God? What robs you of your joy in God? Then base your daily decisions on God-breathed knowledge and Christ-shaped character.

Die daily. Put to death what is earthly in you (Colossians 3:5-9).

Get violent against your shortcomings. Relentlessly attack the footholds of Satan and your flesh with the strength that God supplies.

Be honest. Preaching can, at times, be a lonely calling. More than ever before, however, technology can be used in good and constructive ways to encourage and be encouraged. Use the people and resources at your disposal to fend off the discouragement of isolation. Honestly acknowledge and seek spiritual reinforcement for the areas of life where you are being defeated.

> Sometimes, the bravest thing you can do is run. "Flee from sexual immorality"

Be accountable. Tools of accountability—particularly for the fight against online temptations—are readily available; a few of them are free. I have free software installed on every computer I use that monitors all Internet sites I visit. Anything deemed morally questionable or unacceptable is recorded and sent to the two e-mail addresses of my accountability partners twice a month. Accountability breeds integrity.

Preach to yourself. You spend plenty of time preaching to others; take a cue from Psalm 42:5 and preach to yourself! "Why are you cast down, O my soul, and why are you in turmoil within me? Hope in God; for I shall again praise him, my salvation and my God."

Remember the warning of James 3:1. "Not many of you should become teachers, my brothers, for you know that we who teach will be judged with greater strictness." There will simply be no excuses for sexual immorality on the great day when God brings "every deed into judgment, with every secret thing, whether good or evil" (Ecclesiastes 12:14).

Don't be afraid to retreat. We don't generally commend soldiers for their strength and courage when they run away as the battle reaches its boiling point, but this is a different kind of battle against a different kind of enemy. Sometimes, the bravest thing you can do is run. "Flee from sexual immorality" (1 Corinthians 6:18).

Celebrate victories. Unashamedly and consistently exult in what God has done in your life. "The LORD is my rock and my fortress and my deliverer, my God, my rock, in whom I take refuge, my shield, and the horn of my salvation, my stronghold. I call upon the LORD, who is worthy to be praised, and I am saved from my enemies" (Psalm 18:2-3).

Learn from defeats. Everyone falls. Every man suffers defeat from time to time. But the man of integrity makes the effort to learn so that he might avoid repeating the mistakes of the past. Analyze the weak spots. When are you most vulnerable to temptation? Sharpen your spiritual senses to the triggers that have led to past downfalls. Only the fool ignores such things.

Take the time to refresh yourself. "Finally, brothers, whatever is true, whatever is honorable, whatever is just, whatever is pure, whatever is lovely, whatever is commendable, if there is any excellence, if there is anything worthy of praise, think about these things" (Philippians 4:8). It's easy to become so consumed with next Sunday's sermons and the midweek class material and the home Bible studies and the hospital visits that we fail to adequately feed and refresh ourselves. Don't allow your own soul to shrivel out of personal negligence. A beat-down, worn-out, shriveled soul plus a sudden seductive temptation will end in spiritual disaster more often than not.

Recognize and destroy the idolatry in your life. Sex is a gift, a wonderful blessing of our Creator. But the gift of sex is not greater than the Giver. Enjoy His good gift in the way He has prescribed. But even then, don't be so enamored with the gift that you fail to give complete allegiance to the Giver. Such is idolatry, defection, and betrayal against the One who matters most of all.

I'm praying for you, brothers. Please pray for me. Let's keep our focus sharp, our courage strong, and our eyes on the King. May He be glorified in us—in public and behind closed doors.

{See Jason Hardin's website for more information on these subjects: **www.InGodsImage.com**}

The Preacher's Temptation to Commit Adultery
Edwin Crozier

Fred turned the key in the ignition. After the car sputtered to life, he slumped against the steering wheel and cried. "God, I'm sorry. I don't know how this happened." He was leaving Betty's house; tonight's "Bible study" had turned into fornication. While it was happening, it seemed amazing. It felt so right. It felt like what he knew he had deserved for so long. But now that it was over, his heart was a jumbled mess of guilt and shame; his mind was a jumbled mess of trying to figure out how on earth this happened but at the same time asking, "What did you expect?" The last three "studies" had ended with them kissing. "What did you think would happen if you kept getting together?" he asked himself as he pulled onto the highway that stretched between Betty's house and his own. A semi was speeding down the road in the opposite direction. For a brief moment he considered turning his car to hit it head on, but he couldn't bring himself to do it. He took the long way home and stopped at a gas station to straighten his clothes and check for any telltale signs. He hoped he had stayed out late enough that his wife would already be asleep. He was wrong. He tried to behave nonchalantly when he entered, but as he walked through the door, his wife smiled and said, "I kept dinner warm for you." He blew up at her. He was certain there was accusation of wrong doing in her tone of voice. She went to bed crying, wondering what she had said wrong this time. He stayed up late, too ashamed to go to bed with his wife, wondering what on earth he could possibly preach about this Sunday after what he had done. When he finally went to bed, he couldn't sleep. What if someone found out? What if his wife found out? What if his elders found out? "I'll never do it again," he assured himself as he tossed in the bed. He was wrong.

Sometimes it seems I hear a new story every month—another preacher (or elder) caught fornicating. Parts of the story are different. Sometimes the affair was with a woman; sometimes a man. Sometimes it was a one-time fall; sometimes the preacher had repeatedly fallen. Sometimes the woman seduced the preacher; sometimes the preacher was using his power as a preacher to sexually abuse women or even minors. Sometimes his wife leaves him; sometimes she stays. Sometimes he quits preaching; sometimes he doesn't. Sometimes the preacher goes on with life; sometimes the preacher goes to jail or worse, commits suicide.

How do the rest of us preachers respond? Granted, some compassionately mourn a fallen brother, taking the circumstance as a warning in our own lives. Some, however, respond with, "I'm glad I wasn't the one caught. But I'm thankful for this sign. I'll never commit fornication, look at pornography, or stimulate myself again." Even worse, some respond saying, "Well, I know I'm not perfect, but at least I've never done that." But perhaps the worst, "I just don't understand how any preacher could do that. I know I never will." As if to emphasize the point, we punish our congregations with haranguing, practically accusatory, sermons for weeks about the awfulness of fornication. Sometimes, we end up being the next story everyone hears about.

> I think Satan is waiting around to hear us say, "I'll never do that." That seems to be his cue to try to prove us wrong.

It Can Happen to Me

Paul wrote, "Therefore let anyone who thinks that he stands take heed lest he fall" (I Corinthians 10:12). I think Satan is waiting around to hear us say, "I'll never do that." That seems to be his cue to try to prove us wrong.

"God, I thank you that I am not like other men, extortioners, unjust, adulterers..." (Luke 18:11). How many times have we quoted this verse in classes and sermons? Yet, how many times have we essentially said, "God, I thank you that I didn't commit fornication like that preacher"? When we're talking to other preachers we nod knowingly about how awful it is and say, "How could they do that?"

They do that because Satan is a roaring lion seeking someone to devour (1 Peter 5:8). They do that because sin deceives, destroys and dominates (Romans 7:10-24). They do that because our enemy is cunning, baffling, and powerful. I'm not making excuses for them. I'm not claiming they are not responsible for their sins. I'm not saying, "The devil made them do it; cut them some slack." I'm sure some preachers who fornicated were just wicked hypocrites, intent on using their status as a preacher to cover their sins. However, I'm equally sure that most have done this because they were certain they never would and sin took up the challenge to prove them wrong. They thought they were powerful enough to take Satan on. They were mistaken.

If they were mistaken, I might be too. If sin could do that to them, what can it do to me? Instead of allowing the fall of a brother to be an opportunity to glory in my own power, I need to let it be a warning of sin's power. It needs to be a reminder that if I don't crucify myself (Galatians 2:20) and take up my cross today (Luke 9:23), I might be the next story.

> Instead of allowing the fall of a brother to be an opportunity to glory in my own power, I need to let it be a warning of sin's power.

The Root Problem is Lust

James said, "Each person is tempted when he is lured and enticed by his own desire. Then desire when it has conceived gives birth to sin, and sin when it is fully grown brings forth death" (James 1:14-15). What causes sexual sin? Sexual lust. No wonder Jesus warned us against lust saying, "Everyone who looks at a woman with lustful intent has already committed adultery in his heart" (Matthew 5:28). Usually we think about that statement as an accusation; we should also think of it as a warning. If we've already committed adultery with a woman in our hearts a dozen times, what are we likely to do when given the opportunity? Commit adultery with her in our beds.

Notice what Paul said about lust in Romans 7:7-24. I find it interesting that while making a general point about sin he used coveting/lusting as his example, and what a perfect example it is. The law said, "You shall not covet." But sin used the commandment as an opportunity to deceive and produced all kinds of coveting. Remember that one of the kinds of coveting was coveting your neighbor's wife (Exodus 20:17). Paul said through this deception, sin killed him. It deceived and destroyed him. That, however, was not the worst part. Lust was not satisfied with simply destroying him. It had to dominate him. "I do not understand my own actions. For I do not do what I want, but I do the very thing I hate. Now if I do what I do not want, I agree with the law, that it is good. So now it is no longer I who do it, but sin that dwells within me" (Romans 7:15-17).

If we give lust an inch, it will take us a light year. It is not satisfied with simply causing us to sin. It wants to dominate our lives. We will vow to stop repeatedly, but our enslavement will take over. We'll do what we hate. We won't understand how it keeps happening. Even worse, it won't be satisfied keeping us merely at the point of committing fornication in our hearts. If left unchecked it will eventually carry us to fornication with our bodies. This is a spiritual law as much as gravity is a physical one. We can no more let lust have a part of our lives and avoid sexual immorality than we can jump off the Empire State Building and avoid splatting on the ground.

How Does It Happen?

Let's get rid of simplistic ideas. It doesn't happen simply because we don't love our wives or God. Yes, yes, I know when we define love as an action of obeying God we can make the semantic argument that a fornicator "by definition" doesn't love God or his wife. However, we need to understand that there are plenty of preachers who care deeply about God and their wives and yet they commit this sin. If you don't believe me, let me ask you about your sins. Does your pride, your gossiping, your lying, your drinking, your coveting, your outbursts of anger, your whatever sin it is you've committed mean you don't care deeply about God or your wife? Does it help you overcome the sins you've committed to just be told over and over again, "You need to love God and your wife more"? Then stop tossing that simplistic cliché at folks who are struggling with a different sin (or maybe the same sin).

Additionally, it doesn't happen because the person just hadn't been told enough how wrong it was. They don't need to hear another sermon that claims "God will judge the sexually immoral and adulterous" (Hebrews 13:4). Those preachers who have committed fornication have likely preached some of the best sermons on the subject. After all, they were trying to convince themselves to stop.

How does it happen? In baby steps. No emotionally, mentally, and spiritually healthy person wakes up one morning and says, "Today, I think I'll commit adultery." It starts with lust. It leads to fantasy. It turns into isolation. It breeds guilt and shame, which deepen the cycle. It cuts off intimacy with the right people. It turns to sex with self. It causes gaping emotional holes. It opens the door to pornography. It starts to groom women in the congregation, the neighborhood, or the family. It opens an emotional door with someone. An opportunity arises. The adultery strikes.

No two stories are exactly alike, and yet every story is essentially the same. Usually it involves several key issues.

1) *An unhealthy view of sexuality*: Butch Hancock, country music artist and songwriter, supposedly said, "Life in Lubbock, Texas, taught me two things: One is that God loves you and you're going to burn in hell. The other is that sex is the most awful, filthy thing on earth and you should save it for someone you love." Regrettably, many Christians, and therefore preachers, enter marriage with this or some other unhealthy concept of sex. It may have been because their parents didn't tell them the truth about sexuality. It may have been because a parent, stepparent, sibling, uncle, aunt, grandparent, neighbor, teacher, preacher abused them sexually. It may have been because their curiosity got the better of them and they experimented outside the bounds of God's glorious plan for sex. They know fornication is wrong, but they don't know what sex is really all about. A lot of fornicators think the problem is with their wives. "If only she would have sex with me more…" Maybe there is a preacher out there with healthy views of sex that simply married a woman who won't have sex enough and who has turned to adultery. However, if there are such preachers, I tend to think that number can be counted on one hand. Usually, unhealthy views of sex cause a downward spiral for sex in marriage. Brothers, if you bring unhealthy sex into your marriage, don't be surprised when your wife isn't all that interested in sex with you.

2) *Emotional disconnect*: The "White Book," the manual for Sexaholics Anonymous, describes "The Problem" saying, "Many of us felt inadequate, unworthy, alone, and afraid. Our insides never matched what we saw on the

outsides of others. Early on, we came to feel disconnected—from parents, from peers, from ourselves."[1] Add to that the disconnected feeling from God. Because of whatever caused the unhealthy views of sexuality, some sever their connections with others and turn inward. Of course, many maintain outward shallow connections. They have friends. They are married. They "go to church." But they don't have deep meaningful relationships. They are disconnected and alone.

3) *Medication and Escape*: At some point, something sexual happens. They see the underwear ads in a clothing catalogue, see their first naked woman in a movie, find a family member's porn stash, stumble across a sexual website, hear about sex with self and try it, or start dating and do what "feels right." It is so amazing and makes them feel so good that the next time they feel bad, they naturally turn to it. It becomes a means of escape. Is reality just too much for them to handle? Then fantasy will make it all better. Are they in trouble? Turn to lust. Are they sad? Something sexual will help. Are they angry or stressed? Sex with self will calm their nerves. Are they happy or glad? Sex is the way to celebrate. Like an alcoholic, they can't handle the feelings, but instead of drink, they turn to the sexual to numb the emotions.

4) *Guilt and shame set in*: Perhaps they were already Christians when all this started. Maybe they were already preachers. Maybe they became a Christian or a preacher after these cycles had already begun (sadly some become preachers out of a misguided attempt to pay for these very sins). Either way, the guilt and shame from knowing the truth about their actions simply increased the need for medication and escape. Something happened and they turned to the sexual to escape. Then they feel worse. They claim they will never do it again, but the guilt and shame from their sin makes reality too hard to deal with and in no time they are sinning again.

5) *Fear of intimacy*: We see the vicious cycle. Lack of intimacy breeds unhealthy lust and sex; unhealthy sex breeds lack of intimacy. In fact, if your sexual experiences are unhealthy, even if they are in marriage, they counteract intimacy. They destroy the connection. Sadly, some men have convinced themselves as long as they are having sex with their wives they are okay. However, for some, even sex with their wives is part of the problem.

They have no emotional connection with her. They are simply in it for the orgasm, the personal feeling, the sensation, the sexual hit. Then they roll over and go to sleep. At some point, they can't do anything but this because they just don't know how to be intimate. They aren't really becoming one flesh with their wives, because what they are doing is not really about being with their wives. They are afraid to become truly one with another so they settle for Satan's mediocre copy of God's great gift. God offers emotional, mental, and spiritual unity celebrated in physical union with someone committed to love, but they have opted simply for a moment of physical pleasure.

6) *Escalation*: As I said, this happens in baby steps. Lust and sexual immorality will escalate. Remember, sin is not happening simply to kill us; it wants to dominate us. It will take us further than we ever thought we would go and cause us to do things we never thought we would. For a time, some preachers will think they aren't harming anyone because their sin is simply lust. Maybe it is just pornography, but no one has to know. Maybe they are compulsively having sex with self, but at least they aren't committing adultery. If this behavior continues, it will lead to adultery sooner or later. If you are telling yourself you have it under control and it will never get to that, then try stopping the behaviors you're participating in now. If you can't seem to do that, you are not the one in control—the sin is.

7) *Seeking connection with someone else*: This is where there is a divergence. Some preachers, not knowing how to be intimate, but having become enslaved to fantasy and sexual release, cave to impersonal sex. They frequent strips clubs, erotic massage parlors, anonymous sex, prostitutes, one night stands on trips (even Gospel meetings), etc. Others, seeming to have stronger willpower, don't cave to those sins. Rather, they continue to struggle internally. They fight the "private" sins until one day a seeming connection is made with someone—a neighbor, a family friend, a member of the church. The next thing they know they are committing fornication. Perhaps it is with an adult; maybe it is a child. Sin has taken over. The process has blinded them. Some purposefully and others unwittingly are now not only guilty of immorality but even psychological abuse.

I have no doubt some of you are saying, "this can't be right." Surely some folks just slipped directly into adultery. I'm not omniscient. There may be some cases in which some preacher just got hit with a temptation out of left field and slipped directly into adultery. However, I'm convinced there aren't very many of those and that most of those preachers who explain their sexual sins this way are probably deceiving or deceived themselves.

How Do I Overcome the Temptation?

I've had two sips of alcohol in my life. Being told, "Don't drink alcohol," pretty much did the trick. I've never had to ask, "How do I overcome the temptation to drink alcohol?" because it's just not that much of a temptation (I say this with a great amount of caution because I know Satan and sin are listening). Lust is a different story for me. It is one of the four horsemen of my own personal apocalypse (the others are gluttony, covetousness, and pride). For me it has taken a whole lot more than being told, "No," with a slap on the wrist and a good sermon to fight the battle with lust. Telling myself and being told by others, "Just don't do it," never worked. With that in mind, understand I'm

> Get accountability partners. Read your Bible. Keep your computer in a public place. Don't be alone with a woman that isn't your wife.

not really writing to those who haven't ever had a problem with this issue. If you haven't, then follow the common advice. Get accountability partners. Read your Bible. Keep your computer in a public place. Don't be alone with a woman that isn't your wife. You should be okay. However, if you have committed adultery, or if, like me, lust has been a major problem and you know you've started walking the path that will lead to adultery, then this section is for you. If you are really asking how do I overcome the temptation to lust and adultery, I can promise you it will take more than just boosting your willpower and hearing another sermon.

I'll share what has helped me:

Help #1: Realize you can't overcome. That is the message of Romans 7:14-25. Whenever Paul relied on himself, his own commitment, his own willpower, he ended up doing the very thing he hated. No wonder he uttered the despairing cry, "Wretched man that I am! Who will deliver me from this body of death?" However, he had an answer. "Thanks be to God through Jesus Christ our Lord!" God could deliver him through Jesus Christ. This did not just mean being delivered from the guilt of sin. This meant being delivered from the sin. If you keep thinking all you have to do is try harder next time, you'll just fall harder. There is only one path out of sin's enslavement and that is by the grace of God, not your strength. Your strength got you mired in the mess. Jesus said, "Blessed are the poor in spirit, for theirs is the kingdom of heaven" (Matthew 5:3). Too often we live that passage in the past tense. "I was poor in spirit, that's why I committed all those sins in the past. Now I'm pretty rich and strong in my spirit. I've got it under control." However, the passage is in the present tense. You must still recognize your poverty of spirit. You need to understand how little you can accomplish in the face of sin even now. As long as you think you've really got it under control or you can get it under control if you try harder, you'll always fail. Only when you come to grips with the fact that God's grace is sufficient and your strength isn't, will you really start to overcome (2 Corinthians 12:7-10).

Help #2: Realize God's way works. Jesus also said, "Blessed are the meek, for they shall inherit the earth" (Matthew 5:5). That is, blessed are those who, having recognized they can't win the battle, surrender, and submit themselves to the control of God. Blessed are those who do not try to assert their own will and way, but rather walk the narrow path of God. Sadly, many people give shallow advice when telling those who struggle with this sin to quit. "When the temptation comes, sing a song, read the Bible, quote a memory verse." Obviously these are great things to do. However, usually the motivation is wrong. Most Christians think, "If I just pray more, read my Bible more, sing more, spend more time with Christians, I'll be strong enough to overcome." Usually, these disciplines seem to help for a while, but the crash inevitably comes. Why doesn't this work? Who are you still relying on? You. You're trying to be strong enough. You're trying to be good enough. Stop that. Instead, follow God's way. Why read your Bible, pray, or connect with other Christians? So it will make you strong enough? So you can prove you're good enough? No. Do these things because God's way works. If you want to overcome lust and adultery, you can only do it if you surrender to God. These things don't make you strong enough or good enough. They simply connect you to the God who can deliver you. If you are reading your Bible now more than ever in an effort to be strong enough, it won't last. If however, you are reading the Bible today because you know unless you connect to God you'll fail, that will help.

Help #3: Half measures avail nothing. Jesus said, "If your right eye causes you to sin, tear it out and throw it away…If your right hand causes you to sin, cut it off and throw it away" (Matthew 5:29-30). If lust is leading you to adultery or if you've already committed adultery, you have to start cutting things

> **Lust always starts small and builds.**

off and throwing things away. Quit justifying Google searches for images to put on your PowerPoint presentations without heavy filtering software, if at all. You may have to move to get away from the person you connected with. Don't try to control and enjoy lust. Don't think you can take in a little lust with the television show that shows some lust triggering images. If you find that something arouses you and turns on your lust, you have to get rid of it. Lust always starts small and builds.

"But if I take such drastic measures, I'm afraid someone will learn of my struggle." And? "But if they learn, my wife might leave me, my elders may fire me, folks may look down on me." Now we are at the heart of it. Jesus said, "Blessed are those who hunger and thirst for righteousness, for they shall be satisfied" (Matthew 5:6). If you hunger for marriage, a preaching job, everyone else's praise and adoration, then take half-measures with your lust and adultery. However, understand this. Your lust will not be satisfied. Everything you put before your battle with lust will eventually be lost. Do you honestly think your marriage will survive if you continue pursuing lust? Do you honestly think your role as a preacher will be able to go on long term if you keep lust alive? Your lust will cost you those things anyway. This is a hard saying, but if you want to overcome lust and adultery you have to be willing to do whatever it takes. This is about you and your relationship with God, wife or no wife, preaching or no preaching, adoration of others or no adoration of others. It may be that we lose everything we previously valued as we fight this battle, but we have to ask, "What will it profit us if we gain the whole world but forfeit our soul? Or what shall we give in return for our soul?" (cf. Matthew 16:26).

Help #4: Take it one day at a time. In Luke 9:23, Jesus said, "If anyone would come after me, let him deny himself and take up his cross daily and follow me." Carrying the cross is not something we do for a lifetime, a decade, a year, a month, or even a week. It is something we do for a day. If you get bogged down thinking you must never lust for the rest of your life, you'll be overwhelmed and give up. That's just too hard. Or, you'll do like so many others and think, "Since I'm never going to do this again, one last time won't hurt." Then you'll "last hurrah" your way into the grave. Take it one day at a time. Just work on doing what is right today. You may not even see tomorrow. Why ruin your efforts to glorify God today by your fears that you won't be able to glorify Him tomorrow? Today has enough of its own worries, let tomorrow take care of itself (Matthew 6:34).

Tell God what you are thinking about.

Help #5:Walk in God's presence. Hebrews 13:5 says, "Keep your life free from the love of money, and be content with what you have, for he has said, 'I will never leave you nor forsake you.'" If you believe God is with you, then act like it. While you need specific prayer times, don't just reserve prayer for your prayer closet. Carry on a conversation with God as you go through your day. Tell God what you are thinking about. Tell God what decisions you are trying to make. Ask for His guidance. Thank God for the opportunities to glorify Him. Thank God for the opportunities to learn and grow. When someone cuts you off in traffic, instead of practicing road rage, thank God for the opportunity to practice humility and grace. When you see a triggering woman, tell God about the temptation and ask for strength to look away. Trust me; it's hard to look down a woman's shirt if you're having a conversation with God about it. If you already looked down the woman's blouse, don't give up on your conversation with God; be honest with Him. Confess it. Apologize. Ask for strength and purity. Talk to God about the targets of your lust. Ask Him to provide them the blessings you want. Ask Him to protect them from those who would mentally steal from them and use them. A favorite prayer I've learned when faced with lust's temptation: "God, help me find in You, whatever I'm looking for in _____." Walking in God's presence doesn't work because it is a mind game of thinking God is watching you. It helps because you are seeking the connection with God instead of through lust.

Help #6: Pinpoint what you are trying to escape. When the temptation arises, you pray about it. Get out a journal and start writing down what is going on in your mind. What feelings are you trying to medicate? Are you feeling angry, hurt, lonely, sad, glad, afraid, guilty, ashamed? Then ask what you should really do to face those feelings. I believe this is part of seeking first God's kingdom and righteousness (Matthew 6:33). That is, work on figuring out what the right thing to do is in the face of these emotions. Here's a warning. When you first start taking up the armor of God and fighting against this temptation, you'll feel miserable. Every feeling will be one hundred times stronger than it has been in a long time because you'll no longer be medicating these feelings with lust. Sometimes you'll want to escape back into the captivity of lust just to get back on an even emotional plain. Don't do it. Sit in the feelings. Journal the feelings. Work through how you should really respond. Are you lonely? Don't connect with a prostitute; rather spend time with your wife getting to know her (not having sex with her, but really connecting). Call a brother in Christ and let him know you are lonely and just needed to connect with someone. Are you sad? Write about why. Sometimes you just need to be sad. Call a trusted brother who can weep with you when you weep. Find what you are trying to escape and face it. I can tell you a personal story. I vividly remember a night when I was feeling very triggered in my lust. I called and talked it through with a trusted friend and recognized what I was trying to escape. I had been keeping a secret from my wife that I needed to confess. I got off the phone, went directly to my wife and shared the secret. The lust lost its power. I had pinpointed what I was trying to escape. Instead of escaping, I faced it and by God's strength I was victorious.

Help #7: Cast it out. James 1:16 says, "Therefore confess your sins to one another and pray for one another, that you may be healed." I personally believe that is a spiritual healing. Whether or not you agree, you can see the direction to confess to others. The saying goes, "You're only as sick as your secrets." Find someone you can trust, who is understanding, and will be a source of grace in your life to cast out your sinful secrets. Confess them. Hopefully, this can be your shepherds. Maybe it will be another preacher. Maybe it is a good brother in the congregation. However, this is not simply a cathartic cleanse of dumping your stuff on someone else. Rather, do this as an effort to find a true connection with other people, especially God's people. We often connect to God by connecting to His other children. Sadly, in the church we often isolate ourselves from the very people God has given to help us because we are too mired in our pride. We don't want anyone knowing our weakness and so we are all walking around in some weakness trying to act like everything is okay.

Take this a step further. Don't wait until you've committed a sin to cast it out to someone else. When you are tempted, make a call. Share with that trusted, understanding, gracious person what went through your mind. For me, when I try to stuff something down on the inside and control it, it has a tendency to take over. It is like too much jell-o stuffed in too little of a mold. It will come out somewhere. However, when I share it with someone, letting the light in on it, it loses its power. Sometimes I have to repeatedly call or call multiple people, but letting in the light makes the lust lose its power. Trying to hide it seems to give it strength.

A word here for those who are called in this situation: In most cases, when I make a call like this, I don't need advice. I don't need instruction. I just need understanding. When someone has made the step to make this kind of call, they know the right thing. They don't need a lecture on how they shouldn't lust; they already know that. They don't need you to fix them. They definitely don't need you to sit in judgment over them as if their temptation disgusts you. Who among us can really take that approach? They need an understanding ear that is thankful they are doing the right thing and making the call, encouraging them to continue in what is right.

Help #8: You might want some professional counseling. I say this with trepidation because I know the natural reaction of preachers is to say, "The Bible contains all the help I need." That used to be my reaction. Understand that I'm not suggesting you step away from God's help through His Word. The Bible says, "Without counsel plans fail, but with many advisers they succeed" (Proverbs 15:22). It also says, "Plans are established by counsel; by wise guidance wage war" (Proverbs 20:18). Some folks have been trained to help you deal with this very issue. They know the mental, emotional, physical, and spiritual struggle that is tied up in this battle and they can help. Wage your war by the help of their good counsel. Yes, there are some rotten counselors who will turn you from God. The answer is not to repudiate all counselors. After all, aren't there some rotten preachers out there too? The answer is to make sure the counseling is biblically based. There are even Christians who have become counselors to help with this. Interview the counselor and make sure he will provide help based on scriptural principles. With the help of a good, biblically based counselor you can walk the tangled web of disclosure to your wife, family, shepherds, and others. With his help you can talk through the emotions you have forgotten how to deal with. Don't be ashamed to get help from those who have been specifically and intensely trained to help with this temptation and sin.

Conclusion

As long as any among us continue to sit in judgment saying, "How on earth could anyone do that?" we'll never really wage the war against Satan on this front. Satan is eating us alive with lust and adultery. It's going to take more than good sermons to overcome this battle. It's going to take some radical honesty with each other and all out war against the flesh to win this battle. Let's learn to fight this fight together or many of us will die alone behind the preacher's door.

[1] Sexaholics Anonymous, SA Literature, Nashville, TN, 1989-2002, p v.
{See Edwin Crozier's website for more information on these subjects: http://edwincrozier.com}

The Preacher's Money
David A. Banning

Every morning my co-worker and I spend an hour or so with the young men who work in our preacher training program. In addition to reading and discussing the biblical text, we also spend time talking about preaching. Our discussions are open to any topic that impacts a preacher's work for the Lord. These conversations cover a variety of subjects, from their questions about the text to preparing PowerPoint slides to maintaining a good relationship with their spouses.

> **Some preachers are irresponsible in the way they handle the support they are given and are plagued with the burden of debt.**

It should come as no surprise that our discussions sometimes find their way to money issues. Conversations like these may not seem as relevant as a good talk about the indwelling of the Holy Spirit, but how a preacher handles his money will certainly impact his work. Money can present a problem for a variety of reasons. Sometimes preachers underestimate the support they need and find themselves struggling to make ends meet. Some are irresponsible in the way they handle the support they are given and are plagued with the burden of debt. Still others fail to act with integrity when faced with financial struggles and destroy their influence. In the end, whether it's the loss of influence or simply the distracting concern of figuring out how to get the bills paid this month, it all impacts our labors for the Lord in a negative way.

It is God's desire that all of His children experience peace (Galatians 5:22-23). But more than simply wanting this for us, God provides through His word the wisdom we need to achieve financial peace. In fact, God speaks in great detail about how we should manage the resources He has placed in our hands. To avoid being distracted from our work or damaging our influence with others, preachers need to take these instructions to heart and live them in their daily walk. To that end, let's consider nine simple strategies that will help us manage our money wisely.

Resist the Materialistic Mindset

Avoiding financial turmoil begins with the mind. It is easy to fall into the trap of materialistic thinking. Some brother pulls up in a brand new car and suddenly we are dissatisfied with our own. We complain to our spouse about how old it is and how bad it looks. We begin to believe that it is unfair that

> Avoiding financial turmoil begins with the mind.

other people have new cars and we do not. After all, we work just as hard as they do. We deserve one too. After a couple of weeks of pouting, we can find ourselves sitting in the finance office at the local Chevy dealer signing up for six years of payments that will take us to the brink of financial crisis. It is this kind of materialistic thinking that gets us into trouble.

When it comes to money and possessions, preachers must get their thinking straight. This is where we begin to win the battle for financial peace. God has a lot to say about our attitude toward money. Jesus said that life is not about money and possessions (Luke 12:13-21). Paul warned that if we let this mindset take over, it will destroy us (I Timothy 6:6-10). What does matter is that we have a relationship with God (Ecclesiastes 12:13-14). If we have this, we have what matters. Everything else is just detail. Sometimes we need to listen to our own sermons on this subject.

Know What You Need

Some preachers (especially younger preachers) put themselves in a bind before they ever receive their first check. They agree to a salary without truly knowing how much they will need. This is especially a problem for men who leave secular jobs with large benefit packages. They calculate living expenses without taking into account things like the high cost of purchasing private health insurance, taxes, retirement, etc. When they begin their local work and the true cost of living begins to hit them, they immediately begin to fall behind and soon face financial crisis.

The solution to this problem is for preachers to know what they need before they agree to a salary. Younger preachers who are just getting started and older men who are leaving secular work need to spend some time talking over finances with men who have been preaching for a while. Draw on their experience to construct a list of expenses you may not be anticipating. Discuss the details of tax law for preachers so you take advantage of every deduction and avoid overpaying your taxes. It is also important to know something about the area in which you will be living (cost of housing, utilities, state income tax, etc.). The cost of living can vary from place to place by $10,000 a year or more. There are several Internet sites that can help you calculate the differences in cost of living. The point is this: before you agree to a salary, you need to have an accurate picture of what you will need to adequately provide for your family.

Don't Take a Vow of Poverty

Even after accurately calculating their cost of living, some preachers get into financial trouble because they settle for the minimum amount that is necessary to pay the bills. This becomes a problem when life fails to follow the budget. What happens when a child needs a prescription that far exceeds what we budgeted for medical expenses? What happens when the refrigerator goes out? What happens when the house needs a new roof? For those living on the minimum, circumstances like these can immediately throw them into financial crisis. If two or three things like this happen at one time, it can lead to financial disaster.

But there is another problem. Settling for the minimum leaves nothing for financial needs that are not part of the monthly bills. Responsible families should be setting aside money each month for savings. Parents need to be saving for college expenses for their children. Couples need to save for that time in life when they will not be able to work. Because these are not "bills" that have to be paid each month, they are often neglected. However, over time this neglect can be financially devastating.

It is certainly true that preachers should adjust their standard of living in order to save for the future. We can settle for a smaller house or a cheaper car in order to set aside money for retirement and an emergency fund. But it is also reasonable to expect churches to consider such needs as they decide on a salary.

Don't Spend More than You Make

> Once a preacher is adequately supported, it becomes his responsibility to handle this money with wisdom.

Once a preacher is adequately supported, it becomes his responsibility to handle this money with wisdom. This brings us to the fundamental law of family finances: Income must exceed expenses. This seems obvious, and yet, it is a truth lost on most Americans. Roughly half of American families spend more money every year than they make.

Society has made it easy to live beyond our means. Credit card companies offer a quick and easy solution when we have too much month and too little money. When we have spent all of our income, we can still buy groceries, pay for gas and even eat out at a restaurant. All we have to do is swipe the credit card and defer payment for another time. Society has also removed the stigma of buying on credit. In past generations people believed that you were supposed to save for the things you wanted. Today, people think nothing of financing lunch at McDonalds. Credit card debt is just accepted as a normal part of family life.

The problem with pushing the consequences of our spending into next month is that, eventually, it catches up with us. As the debt rises, our ability to pay shrinks. Ultimately, we become enslaved (Proverbs 22:7). The only way to avoid this trap is to change the way we do business. We must learn to live within our means.

It is similar to trying to lose weight. If we want to take off a few pounds, then we cannot take in more calories than we burn. There is no way around this law. It doesn't matter what excuses we make ("I deserve two desserts because this is a special occasion"). If we take in more calories than we burn, then we will not lose weight. The same law applies to finances. It doesn't matter what excuses we make ("I need a new suit because I'm performing a wedding" or "We went out to eat so we could spend time with brethren"). If we spend more than we make, we will end up in debt and suffer all the grief that goes with it.

Work from a Budget

The need for a budget actually grows out of the previous point—we cannot spend more than we make. If we are to be successful in our efforts to live within our means, then we must have a budget. Just as the wise man urged shepherds of his day to "know well" the condition of their flocks (Proverbs 27:23-27), so we too must "know well" what is happening with the financial resources committed to our trust.

Husbands and wives must build the budget together.

A budget is simply a plan for properly allocating our money (Proverbs 21:5). This "plan" can come in many different forms. For some it will be a bunch of numbers scratched on a yellow pad. For others it's three pages of an Excel spreadsheet. But no matter which method is used, a budget must have two basic components. It must include a list of all the income for the month and a list all of the expenses for the month. he key to budgeting is making sure that the income number is larger than the expense number. It's not rocket science. However, it is the failure to do this simple exercise every month that leads to financial disaster for many families. We have to prepare a budget. We have to do this every month.

As we work to build a family budget, there are some things we can do that will help us to be successful.

First, the budget must be detailed. We need to record every dollar earned and every dollar spent. It is often the little holes in our budget that get us into trouble. To illustrate, the two dollars we spend every morning for coffee at Starbucks may seem insignificant. However, over the course of the year it becomes a $700 hole. We need to know where that money is going.

Second, husbands and wives must build the budget together. It will not work for one spouse to arbitrarily impose a budget on the other. A wife may have no idea what the family must spend on auto insurance or house maintenance. A husband may not know what his wife has to spend on groceries. This is why we must work together to figure out how the money is going to be spent.

Third, the budget must be honored. Once the budget is set, we have to live by it. To be specific, if we budgeted $100 for eating out this month, then we only spend $100. When that money is gone, we don't eat out. If an unexpected expense arises, we adjust the budget. If our child needs a $100 prescription, then we spend less in other areas to make up the difference, perhaps by giving up a round of golf or spending less on groceries. A husband and wife must come together and make those adjustments. A budget is worthless if we do not stick to it.

Build an Emergency Fund

Sometimes an unexpected expense will far exceed what we can adjust for in the budget. Instead of a $100 prescription, your car may need a $3000 transmission. Cutting back on golf or groceries will not fix this problem. This is why we must be building an emergency fund.

Unexpected expenses will come up. In fact, these are such a regular part of life that it is probably inaccurate to describe them as unexpected. Every year cars break down, refrigerators die, and health insurance premiums increase. Every year we have birthdays, anniversaries, Valentine's Day and Christmas. Sometimes these expected expenses are far more than small financial setbacks. In a given year 34% of American families will be hit with an unexpected expense that will seriously impact their finances. These typically come in the form of major medical expenses or car problems.

Most are completely unprepared for even a small financial setback, much less a big one. When the refrigerator dies or the transmission goes out, they are forced to pay with credit cards. If two or three of these hit at one time, they find themselves in the middle of a debt crisis (Proverbs 22:7).

To avoid this pitfall, families must learn to anticipate the unexpected and plan for it. One way to do this is to build an emergency fund. This is money we set aside in a savings account to pay for emergencies. Your grandmother called this "saving for a rainy day." Experts suggest that you set aside 3-6 months of expenses in this fund. If you have $3,000 in bills every month, you should have no less than $9,000 put away in an emergency fund. This money should remain untouched. It is not extra savings to be spent on a new TV or vacation. It's only for emergencies.

It may not be much fun to have several thousand dollars just sitting around in the bank. However, it dramatically reduces stress in our lives and gives us peace of mind. If the refrigerator dies, we don't have to go into crisis. We draw from the emergency fund and pay for it.

Avoid the Credit Card Trap

One sure way to avoid financial trouble is to minimize the use of credit cards. Purchasing with credit presents a number of problems.

Many do not realize that credit cards are more than simply a way to buy things. There is a whole mentality that goes with them. When we buy on credit, it's as though we are not using real money. As a result, consumers typically spend 15% more when they purchase with plastic. We also tend to lose track of how much we are spending. We buy the things we need or want with little sense of how much is actually going out. When the bill comes at the end of the month, we suffer sticker shock because we had no idea of how much we spent. This does not happen when we operate on a cash system.

Finally, there is something fundamentally unhealthy about spending next month's income thirty days in advance. It makes much more sense to spend September's salary in September. We will serve ourselves well if we will strive to buy with cash. Dave Ramsey recommends the envelope system. At the beginning of the month, put cash into envelopes for different areas of spending based on the amount you budgeted (groceries, eating out, clothing, etc.). For example, if you budgeted $100 for eating out, put $100 in an envelope and label it "eating out." When you go to a restaurant, pull out the envelope and pay with cash. When the envelope is empty, you don't eat out any more that month.

There is some value in hanging on to a credit card. It simplifies hotel reservations and car rentals. But to avoid debt, it is best to use it only for these special circumstances. As much as possible, make purchase with cash, checks or check cards.

Buy Health Insurance

Finding affordable health insurance is one of the struggles preachers face. We typically wind up paying a lot for what seems like little coverage. As a result, some preachers decide to gamble and go without coverage. This decision can be financially devastating. Remember that 1/3 of all Americans suffer a major financial setback each year. For many this comes in the form of a health crisis. When we do not have health insurance, a medical crisis can be catastrophic, leaving in its wake hundreds of thousands of dollars in medical bills.

For this reason, it is vital that preachers find some kind of health insurance. For many this ends up being a major medical policy with high deductibles and little coverage for doctor visits and medications. It basically protects us from a serious medical crisis. The smaller monthly medical expenses will have to be built into our budgets. We cannot treat these as surprises. We must set aside money for them. The high deductibles can be covered by the money in our emergency fund.

It can be frustrating to pay a lot of money each month for insurance that seems to pay for nothing. But the risk is far too great to gamble that we will never have a serious problem with our health.

Save for the Future

It may be that preachers never truly retire, but there will certainly come a time when age and health issues will force us to cut back or perhaps stop preaching altogether. There is also the need to make sure our wives will have what they need should we die before they do. Both of these concerns should provoke us to be saving now for these future expenses. Because preachers have no access to a company retirement plan, it is up to us to be disciplined during our working years to set aside money for that time when we cannot work.

The key to retirement savings is to start early and be consistent. This can be difficult during the early years of preaching, but even doing a little bit every month will make a big difference over the long haul. We cannot live for today and ignore tomorrow. We need to be responsible. We must anticipate the financial needs that will come with our declining years and prepare now to provide for ourselves.

In God's word we find the wisdom we need to avoid these financial pitfalls.

Few things in life cause more stress than worries about money. For those who preach, such stress has an unavoidable impact on our work. In God's word we find the wisdom we need to avoid these financial pitfalls. We must learn these truths and discipline ourselves to walk in them as we fight the daily battle to be financially responsible.

The Preacher's Relationship
with Difficult Brethren
By W. Frank Walton

"I have been…in danger of false brethren" (2 Corinthians 11:26). The apostle Paul faced some difficult brethren, which pained his life. So, faithful preachers can expect there will be difficult brethren to face, because we live in a fallen world.

I once received a letter from an agitated brother who did not like something I had written. Among his harsh comments, he said, "this is enough to make a maggot vomit! " Wow! I highlighted in yellow several other inflammatory remarks and returned the letter to him, asking him if he really to meant to say these harsh things. Guess what? He called me and apologized for overreacting. This shows that good-hearted brethren can be touched in their conscience to change.

Paul's Example with the Vexing Corinthian Brethren

Mastering the practical principles of 1 & 2 Corinthians of how Paul effectively dealt with the deeply flawed Corinthian brethren can help us turn around difficult brethren. God's resources are abundantly able to help us cope with any trouble (as summed up in 2 Corinthians 6:1-13).

The Corinthian correspondence is the most detailed look inside a New Testament church. They were deeply troubled because they were deeply "carnal" (1 Corinthians 3:1-2). "Jealousy" and "strife" ensued (1 Corinthians 3:3; cf. Galatians 5:19-21).

What were their specific problems? In 1 Corinthians, the brethren were divided into cliques over favorite preachers (1:10-13). They were enamored with worldly, Greek philosophy and following men (1:18-3:4, 4:8-10). They arrogantly tolerated a member living in incest (5:1-13). They started lawsuits to resolve religious matters (6:1-8). Some promoted sexual immorality as like a natural desire for food (6:12-20). They were troubled about marital problems (7:1-40), had conflicts and misunderstandings over eating meats offered to pagan idols (8:1-13, 10:23-33) and temptations relative to idolatry (10:1-22). Women removed their veils in worship, which had cultural significance at Corinth of female insubordination (11:2-16). They had disruptive observances of the Lord's Supper (11:17-34). Spirituals gifts engendered competitive jealousy and confusion, with some assertive women speaking out of turn (12:1-14:40). Some taught there was no resurrection, denying the key doctrine of Christ's resurrection (15:12). Instead of giving up on them, Paul planned to visit and stay with them, in order to strengthen them (16:6). What preacher today would like to move to such a work?

Also, 2 Corinthians shows problems remained at Corinth. Still, Paul did not give up. He had made a "painful" second visit to deal with unresolved problems from the first letter (2 Corinthians 2:1; cf. 12:14, 13:1). What had changed in the church? I deduce that the incestuous brother specified for discipline in 1 Corinthians 5:3-5 is the one disciplined by the majority in 2 Corinthians 2:6. He had sinned against Paul (2 Corinthians 2:10, 7:12). It seems most of the Corinthians had repented of the problems in 1 Corinthians, as well as the rebellion against Paul's apostolic authority (2 Corinthians 7:9-11). So, I infer that this sin against Paul was the incestuous brother, who retaliated against Paul for being publicly rebuked by him, thereby introduced "false apostles" (2 Corinthians 11:3) into the Corinthian church. These subsequently misled the church and attacked Paul's apostolic ministry. In 2 Corinthians, Paul explains his sincere motives for ministry (2 Corinthians 1-7). Then, after reminding them of their promise to help needy saints in Jerusalem (2 Corinthians 8-9), Paul takes on the false teachers to defend his apostleship work for Christ (2 Corinthians 10:1-12:18).

Why did God preserve all this "dirty laundry" in the lengthy Corinthian correspondence? In four letters (1 Corinthians 5:9, 2 Corinthians 2:1-4) and three trips (2 Corinthians 12:14, 13:1), all this being compressed in a few years (Acts 18:1-20:3), Paul shows how to effectively deal with problems in the local church. Imperfect brethren have problems, some very deeply ingrained, but the gospel message has the power to either eventually work through these problems or repudiate them in corrective church discipline (1 Corinthians 5:6, 13; 2 Corinthians 12:20-21).

It's Still a Tough World Out There…With Some Brethren's Help

I've heard various preachers' horror stories in dealing with some brethrens' bad behavior. I've experienced some of this too. When I moved to one church, a sister told me, "This church is doctrinally conservative but morally liberal. If you knew what was going on behind the scenes, you would pack your bags and move back." Another sister spent several years staring at the side wall during my sermons (because she could not stand to even look at me), along with shuffling through her purse, grousing out loud about the lesson, etc. When I called to try to resolve the problem, she ended up hanging up the phone. This was an elder's wife!

> I once mentioned in a sermon that I was an imperfect preacher, and a vexing brother said, "Amen!"

In twenty-seven years of preaching, I've had to deal directly with individual brethren about: pornography, lying, gossiping, boozing it up in bars, profanity, unscriptural divorce, adultery, teens disrespectfully cutting up in Bible class, obnoxious and disruptive chatter during public worship, bizarre doctrines about the Godhead, the neglect of corrective church discipline, etc. I had to face an elder, in the presence of the other elders, to give biblical reasons why he should resign due to his inability to do an elder's work. (The other elders concurred he should resign but didn't want to tell him to his face.) I've twice had elders apologize to me, after I had left, that they were sorry they had not dealt with problems. In addition, I sat in a business meeting when a hot-headed brother threw out a proposal to fire me, which upset most of the brethren. These difficulties will also affect a preacher's family. My wife had to endure continually being bad-mouthed behind her back by a deacon's wife, who would hypocritically smile to her face. This member said to another deacon's wife, "I can't stand her, and I don't know why." When confronted in an effort to resolve it, she denied it but later continued this trashing of my wife. Yes, we live in an imperfect world. We all are beset by various sins and weaknesses, which include our own personal foibles. (I once mentioned in a sermon that I was an imperfect preacher, and a vexing brother said, "Amen!").

Yet, preaching is the great work of saving precious souls, for whom Christ died. We are privileged to serve the Lord by being on the front lines of helping imperfect brethren, as well as ourselves, go to heaven. A dedicated preacher can draw closer to Jesus and continue to serve the brethren's spiritual welfare by teaching and modeling the gospel, without becoming disillusioned. A minority of brethren cause a majority of problems in the local church. The vast majority of the Lord's people are the most wonderful people on earth.

Practical Principles from Paul's Example with Corinth

Corinth was a transient, prosperous port city. It was a cesspool of sin in the sinful Roman world. Sexual perversity was so rampant at Corinth that Aristophanes coined the Greek verb *korinthiazomai* (to act the Corinthian) that was synonymous with sexual license (*Fragmenta 354*). Corinth was home of the Temple of Aphrodite, serviced by 1,000 Temple prostitutes. Also, pagan Greek philosophy enveloped Corinth.

Today, we're all surrounded by a corrosive, fallen world that can weaken any among us. A preacher told me that in 10 years at a congregation, he had to deal with 10 cases of adultery. There are no perfect churches, and if there were, preachers would not be needed. Where do we begin?

1. Love Looks for the Good. We must preach out of love for souls, as well as love for God and love for the truth. Paul concluded 1 Corinthians, which had rebuked their many sins, *"My love be with you all in Christ Jesus"* (1 Corinthians 16:24; cf. 4:2; 2 Corinthians 2:4). He urged the troubled church, *"Pursue love....Let all you do be done in love"* (1 Corinthians 14:1, 16:14). He genuinely saw them as his *"beloved brethren"* (1 Corinthians 15:58, 2 Corinthians 7:3). In the second epistle, he opined with broken-hearted love, *"I will most gladly spend and be expended for your souls. If I love you more, am I to be loved less?* (2 Corinthians 12:15; cf. 10:14, 11:11). He was not arrogantly miffed that the Corinthians did not seem to fully appreciate him. He was gladly "spent" for them, if it helped to rescue their soul. He always affirmed his love for them, without which service is nothing (1 Corinthians 13:1-3). Expressing genuine love helps to lower brethren's defense shields and be more accepting of correction. If we do *"everything...in love"* (1 Corinthians 16:14), then we discover, as Dee Bowman pointed out to me years ago, that "love is what makes you real" (*The Velveteen Rabbit*).

Love is sacrificial goodwill to meet the highest good of another. A mark of *agape* love is: not based on the merits of the object of love, but like God, is based on the character of the lover and the need of the one loved. Love's "unconquerable benevolence" (Barclay) is the divine motivation to deal with and help resolve difficulties (1 John 4:7-21). Love is optimistic in dealing with brethren (1 Corinthians 13:7-8a). Paul confidently believed in their potential in Christ: *"who will confirm you to the end, blameless in the day of our Lord Jesus Christ"* (1 Corinthians 1:8). Love will treat people in view of what they can become, not what they have been at their worst moment.

> **Expressing genuine love helps to lower brethren's defense shields and be more accepting of correction.**

Paul's love grew from his connection in helping convert many of them to Christ crucified, the Savior of sinners (Acts 18:8; 1 Corinthians 2:2, 15:1-4). They "were" vile sinners, such as homosexuals and transvestites (1 Corinthians 6:9-10), but no longer! They were *"sanctified in Christ Jesus... in everything you were enriched in Him"* (1 Corinthians 1:2, 5). We need to appreciate where people have come from and what they've had to overcome to be a Christian. People don't become what they are overnight, and they will not be perfected overnight either.

Paul lovingly affirmed the good in them, *"I thank my God always concerning you for the grace of God which was given you in Christ"* (1 Corinthians 1:4; cf. 2 Corinthians 1:11-12). He didn't see only their flaws. The only hope to change sinners into saints is the "grace of God." He appreciated the good they were doing in keeping the apostolic traditions (1 Corinthians 11:2).

Because Paul saw good in them, he challenged them to do right:

to *"follow Christ"* (1 Corinthians 11:2, 6:17), to be a holy *"temple of God"* (1 Corinthians 3:16-17), to work out their inner conflict (1 Corinthians 6:1, 5), to outgrow immaturity (1 Corinthians 14:20), and to do *"all things decently and in order"* (1 Corinthians 14:40). They could do this because they were a *"living letter"* written by the Spirit on their hearts (2 Corinthians 3:3).

What was the result? The majority of the Corinthian brethren repented (2 Corinthians 7:9-10)! Paul expressed great appreciation for their change (2 Corinthians 7:4-16). Some difficult brethren are simply immature or in the process of refining their character flaws. I've seen troubled Christians grow stronger and/or mellower over time. I've seen one brother, who was caught up in homosexuality for over ten years, repent and come back to the Lord because truth could still touch his heart. Others are incorrigible, like the man living with his father's wife (1 Corinthians 5:1-13), who need strong medicine of the public rebuke of corrective church discipline to wake them up (1 Corinthians 5:5).

When we mine for gold, we don't look for just dirt; rather, we look for the precious gold hidden in the dirt. Robert Turner observed that if a preacher "expects perfection or nothing, he will get nothing. Such an attitude can blind him to his own sins and cause him to despise others (Luke 18:9-14). Yet, he must keep the perfect standard before himself and others and work *with* them toward that goal" (*What It Is, Is Preaching, page 141*).

2. Maintain a Christ-like Heart of Patient Service.

Paul is a model of Christ-like service to help brethren grow up in the Lord (1 Corinthians 3:5). Paul's actions were calculated, not to make himself look good, but to serve the Corinthians' best interest. He assured the recalcitrant church, *"It is in the sight of God that we have been speaking in Christ; and all for your upbuilding, beloved"* (2 Corinthians 12:9; cf. 10:8, 13:10). He was a selfless servant, even if his critics put the worst spin on his actions (2 Corinthians 1:17, 23). Paul's servant's heart is revealed in his motivation: *"not that we lord it over your faith but are workers for your joy"* (2 Corinthians 1:24).

Sometimes a preacher is personally hurt by thoughtless, mean-spirited brethren. He can lose his tender, loving heart and become cynical and allow his hurts to angrily seep out in his preaching. It comes across as "fussing at the brethren," instead of preaching "to" their welfare.

Preachers, as an example of Christian service, must die to self and model selfless humility as a slave of Jesus Christ (1 Corinthians 4:1-11). In 1 Corinthians 4:1, Paul said he was Christ's *"servant"* (*Gr. huperetes,* lit. "an under rower" as a slave on a galley ship). He did not see himself as a "big name preacher." He was not *"anything"* of great consequence (1 Corinthians 3:7), because spiritual growth only comes from God (1 Corinthians 3:6). Paul saw himself as just an *"earthen vessel"* (a clay jar) that had the privilege of carrying the precious gospel "treasure" (2 Corinthians 4:7). He had no ego to bruise, because he had died with Christ. So, he didn't care if he was critiqued (1 Corinthians 4:3). *"We preach not ourselves but Christ Jesus as Lord and ourselves as your bondservants for Jesus' sake"* (2 Corinthians 4:5). He would gladly forego personal privileges and rights to help the brethren advance the cause of Christ (1 Corinthians 9:12, 19, 22, 23). He always held out the hope of reconciling their differences (2 Corinthians 6:11-13, 7:2).

In serving the welfare of brethren, ministers must engage in humble introspection (1 Corinthians 4:4, 2 Corinthians 13:5). In dealing with difficult brethren, I must honestly ask myself, "Am I part of the problem?" We're still a work in progress, with various flaws to overcome (cf. Philippians 1:15, 17). So, if we have a prideful, overbearing ego, it will surely expose itself in conflict with brethren. Remember that John Mark experienced temporary failure in preaching (Acts 13:13, 15:38), but he learned from his shortcoming and later became a very useful preacher (1 Peter 5:13, 2 Timothy 4:11). We should see our problems as our teachers to refine our character (James 1:2-4).

3. Humbly Depend on the Lord and Not Self. God's spiritual power is abundantly able to cope with any problem: *"as servants of God, in much endurance, in afflictions, in hardships, in distresses…in purity, in knowledge, in patience, in kindness, in the Holy Spirit, in genuine love, in the word of truth, in the power of God"* (2 Corinthians 6:4, 6-7). Paul depended on the Lord, despite massive challenges. This is why he was *"sorrowful yet always rejoicing"* (2 Corinthians 6:10). See difficulties as a faith building exercise to discover what Paul discovered—God is always sufficient (2 Corinthians 3:5). *The surpassing greatness of the power will be of God and not from ourselves"* (2 Corinthians 4:7).

In fact, Paul's *"thorn in the flesh"* (2 Corinthians 12:7-9), in context, was his difficulties that "weakened" him in preaching (2 Corinthians 12:10; cf. 11:23-33). This "weakness" was an occasion for humble trust in the Lord. *"My grace is sufficient for you, for power is perfected in weakness"* (2 Corinthians 12:9). In our difficulties, we discover Christ's strength to carry on.

Paul said his example was valid only as he would *"follow Christ"* (1 Corinthians 11:2). He encouraged the Corinthians to discover the life-changing power of thinking on the glory of the Lord and being spiritually transformed into His image (2 Corinthians 3:18). Preachers serve the Lord foremost (2 Corinthians 4:5-5:9) and not just to keep a paycheck.

Dealing with difficult brethren can be Christ's opportunity for a preacher to grow as a servant. The apostle Paul said, *"The members of the body which seem to be weaker are necessary"* (1 Corinthians 12:22). Why? It forces us to give them attention to meet their spiritual needs, which is an opportunity to grow in Christ-like service (1 Corinthians 12:23-27). The preacher lives and works for our gracious Savior, in order to help others go to heaven. Paul was patient with his brethren, in order to give them time to develop (2 Corinthians 1:23-24).

4. Focus On Scripture and Not Personalities. Difficulties with brethren are often just carnal personality conflicts. Paul's appeals are rooted in objective truth. He was called *"by the will of God...to preach the gospel"* (1 Corinthians 1:1, 17). *"What matters is the keeping of the commandments of God"* (1 Corinthians 7:19). Our goal should be that it is not *who* is right that matters but *what* is right before the Lord, who will judge us in the end (2 Corinthians 5:10).

I once dealt with a couple undergoing what appeared to be an unscriptural divorce. The sister, bothered about me questioning her, said, "One elder said they had to deal with this because they were being `pressured.'" This was sad news to me, because I had asked the elders what they were going to do about this divorce situation. Elders, preachers, and brethren should deal with problems in the church because of what Scripture commands, not just because somebody objects and "pressures" them to deal with it.

Paul taught the truth for their eternal good (1 Corinthians 5:5; 2 Corinthians 12:19, 10:8, 13:7, 10), not to win a personal argument. Paul was always focused on upholding *"the truth"* (2 Corinthians 13:8), not his personal feelings. A strong biblical appeal is central to growing a healthy church: *"so your faith would not rest on the wisdom of men, but on the power of God"* (1 Corinthians 2:5). Paul begged them to be united *"by the name of our Lord Jesus Christ"* (1 Corinthians 1:10). Divine authority is the standard. A church is only as strong as the Bible teaching that it demands. I once was threatened by an elder with possibly losing my job for preaching the truth on the qualifications of elders. I responded to this veiled threat: "I'll just tell the next preacher that preaching the truth on a sensitive topic may cost him his job, and so what kind of preacher do you think you'll get?"

> A church is only as strong as the Bible teaching that it demands.

In about two dozen instances, Paul rested his case on the quote: *"it is written"* (1 Corinthians 1:19, 31; 2 Corinthians 8:15, 9:9 *et al*). We must ever ask, "What does the Bible say?" Paul insisted that his teaching was not his own but *"the commandments of the Lord"* (1 Corinthians 14:37). He used Old Testament examples to warn of the consequences of ungodly attitudes and actions (1 Corinthians 10:6, 11, 13). Repeated appeals to focus on Scripture and not our feelings can help brethren see that the current issue under discussion is not a mere personal opinion but rather is discovering our responsibility before God. I have seen Scripture pierce the foibles of immature, short-sighted brethren and turn them around. If brethren would just act like Christians, according to the Scriptures, there isn't any problem that couldn't be solved!

5. Confront Sin to Save Souls. The Corinthian correspondence is filled with various sins that Paul specified and admonished to be corrected. If difficulties in the church can be traced to sinful conduct or a wicked character fault, it must be corrected or those impenitent brethren will be condemned on Judgment Day (2 Corinthians 5:10). *"Judge those within the church...Remove the wicked man from among yourselves"* (1 Corinthians 5:12, 13).

So, preachers have front-line responsibility before God and to the brethren to rebuke crying sins in the church (2 Timothy 4:2; cf. Ezekiel

3:17-21). I recall having to confront a deacon in a church who continually "reviled" me behind my back, trying to tear down my work for the Lord. (Paul enumerated a "reviler," along with others sins in 1 Corinthians 5:11, that should not be tolerated in the local church.) When I confronted him about needing to resolve this, he arrogantly quipped, "I don't have to talk to you about anything." Brethren need to realize the biblical duty to resolve all sins in the church.

Paul certainly didn't have the attitude to just teach nice, fluffy lessons and gloss over their damning sins.

At Corinth, Paul's fidelity to truth meant he didn't shy away from dealing with sinful behavior. *"We are ready to punish all disobedience"*(2 Corinthians 11:6). More sins were exposed and rebuked at Corinth than in any other church in the New Testament. Paul identified the underlying condition of many as a lack of dedication to the Lord, being *"weak... sick...asleep"*(1 Corinthians 11:30). He also exposed their underlying carnality, arrogance and worldly thinking (1 Corinthians 3:1-3, 4:6-7, 18; 5:2; 2 Corinthians 10:7). Paul certainly didn't have the attitude to just teach nice, fluffy lessons and gloss over their damning sins.

Moral cowardice fears the trauma of confronting brethren's persistent, pernicious sin. Yet, Paul confidently asserted, in correcting perversions in worship: *"there must be divisions among you, so that those who are approved may become evident"*(1 Corinthians 11:19). Later, he admonished the brethren to *"be separate"* from the bad influence of the false apostles (2 Corinthians 6:14-7:1). Paul's loving honesty exposed the reality of sin. We do no one a favor by allowing them to go to hell with a good conscience.

Paul's teaching on sin did help the majority of the Corinthians to repent and change for the better (2 Corinthians 2:7; 7:9-10). Paul's scriptural warnings against sin were balanced with loving and tender appeals (1 Corinthians 16:24, 2 Corinthians 6:1-3, 11-13). He challenged them, *"Examine yourselves, whether or not if you are in the faith"*(2 Corinthians 13:5). We are all accountable to God for our conduct. *"For we all must stand before the judgment seat of Christ"*(2 Corinthians 5:10). It is the *"fear of the Lord"* that sobers us up to our personal accountability to God and the need to persuade others to turn from sin (2 Corinthians 5:11).

As a preacher, don't let a few bad apples sour you on the great work of preaching. Focus on the many good brethren willing to accept biblical teaching. A lack of consistent church discipline allows a thorny backlog of problems. If the local church clearly shows, over time, that it is too cowardly, lax, or lazy to practice corrective church discipline, then you will be better off going to a church willing to stand for the whole truth. Leave those incorrigible brethren in the hands of the Lord. They may have unfairly opposed your scriptural work, but they have condemned themselves to wickedness.

6. Don't Defend Yourself but Do Defend the Lord's Work Being Done. Paul was very open and vulnerable in dealing with the Corinthians (2 Corinthians 6:11). He also gave a vigorous defense of the scriptural integrity of His apostolic work at Corinth against his critics: *"I will not be put to shame"* (2 Corinthians 10:8). In preaching, we must distinguish between upholding divine truth and a mere personal grievance. Remember, I am not that important but what I am doing for the Lord is eternally important. *"Let no one despise you"* (Titus 2:15).

Paul confronted spiritual error foisted by religious errorist in the church. *"They"* (2 Corinthians 10:10, 11:13-15, 18) were identified as *"false apostles, deceitful workers…ministers of Satan"* (2 Corinthians 11:13-15). He used gospel truth to tear down the fallacy of their worldly tactics (2 Corinthians 10:1-7) and fleshly subjectivism (2 Corinthians 10:12-18). *"We are destroying speculations and every lofty thing raised up against the knowledge of God"* (2 Corinthians 10:5).

Some brethren seem to think that the preacher is paid to be the personal dart- board of disgruntled members. I've had brethren tell me, "You can't stop people from talking about you. Just overlook it." Personal opinions can be overlooked but there are "sins of the tongue" (grumbling, reviling, lying, gossip, etc.) that can damn an impenitent soul to hell and can poison the minds of unsuspecting brethren against the preacher's work. Again, it is the Lord's work done by the preacher that should be defended, not the preacher's personality or feelings.

Allowing ungodly, underhanded tactics to hurt a preacher's work is a corrupting influence in a congregation that professes to stand for the truth and against sin. When there's a conflict, some think the easy answer is: "let's get a new preacher." If the preacher leaves, the unpleasantries of the issue may pass, but the sinful character that reared its ugly head will only be submerged, awaiting the heart-searching, final judgment (2 Corinthians 5:10, 1 Timothy 5:24).

If you must leave a congregation because you have done all you can scripturally do, it is important to not leave by "shooting over your shoulder" (Harold Comer), which is taking cheap shots from the pulpit at the brethren. This helps nothing. The pulpit is no place for snide remarks and petty sniping.

7. Keep a Good Conscience. In dealing with difficult brethren, it is important to not become bitter, cynical, or self-pitying. So, it is imperative in the challenging exercise of dealing with church problems, to maintain a good conscience before the Lord. Paul said, *"I am conscious of nothing against myself"* (1 Corinthians 4:4). While 1 Corinthians is the most intimate view inside a New Testament church, 2 Corinthians is the most intimate view inside a New Testament apostle and his motives. His integrity was above reproach (2 Corinthians 1:12; 2:4, 17). In dealing with troubled brethren, his guiding philosophy was: *"We also have as our ambition, whether at home or absent, to be pleasing to Him"* (2 Corinthians 5:9). Paul disciplined himself like a champion athlete, to keep his eye on running the race faithfully (1 Corinthians 9:24-27). He realized that his work in the Corinthian brethren could be *"burned up"* (lost) but he himself would still be *"saved"* (1 Corinthians 3:15). Just trust that God's plan will work if we will work God's plan.

We can keep our conscience clean by looking to heaven. The problems of this world will not matter in the end. Despite painful circumstances, Paul was *"renewed day by day"* (2 Corinthians 4:16). Whether adversity wears us down or polishes us up depends on what we are on the inside. Look at present difficulties in light of the eternal reward (2 Corinthians 4:16-18). This shrinks our problems down to size and keeps us focused on the big spiritual picture. Paul saw any difficulty as his ally that *"works for us an eternal weight of glory"* (2 Corinthians 4:17). In heaven's light, our problems are *"light"* and *"momentary"* (2 Corinthians 4:16).

Listen to Robert Turner's wisdom from 60 years of preaching: "In the final analysis, the preacher must deal with people. His knowledge of truth and principles will go for naught unless he learns to cope with and apply the message to people" (*What It Is, Is Preaching, page 141*). Mastering the rich contents of 1 & 2 Corinthians in dealing with difficult brethren, Paul's example will strengthen us in effectively doing the glorious work of a faithful evangelist.

The Preacher's Role in the Unity of the Local Church
Russ Bowman

"These six things the LORD hates, Yes, seven are an abomination to Him:...one who sows discord among brethren" (Proverbs 6:19)

On the night of His betrayal, Jesus gathered His apostles together to share a crucial, intimate observance of the Jewish Passover. This must have been an evening full of nervous anticipation, both for the Lord and His apostles, though for different reasons. Jesus had entered Jerusalem five days earlier with a public reception befitting the anticipated Messiah. He had displayed His power and wisdom in the miracles He performed and in His victorious confrontations with the Jewish religious leaders (Matthew 21-23). He had uttered parables and offered prophetic insight into future judgments (Matthew 24-25), and in so doing, fanned the flames of Messianic fervor throughout the city, and particularly among His own disciples. Those eleven faithful men knew that something was going to happen, and it must have been an exciting, but confusing week. Jesus had repeatedly predicted His death, reminding them even during this very week that He would *"be delivered up to be crucified"* on the Passover (Matthew 26:2). Yet they still seemed shocked when it happened. Were they expecting some divine intercession? Did they anticipate that Jesus would change His mind and overpower His enemies? Would they witness the angelic host intervene? Or would they themselves be empowered to rise up against the opposition and deliver their Lord? We are simply not told what they anticipated, though it stands to reason that they were looking for some kind of Messianic drama.

Jesus, on the other hand, must have been concerned for these men. He had convinced them of His Messiahship. They had been given evidence even of His divinity. He had taught them and led them and corrected them and prepared them. And now He was about to leave them. He knew what would happen at His death. He knew they would forsake Him (Matthew 26:31f), knew Peter would deny Him (Matthew 26:34), and knew that they would ultimately stand fast and do the work for which He had prepared them. Yet the next three days would be crushing for them, and Jesus is clearly concerned about them as He gathers them together for the Passover meal. What an example, that the Lord would be so mindful of His followers when faced with the terror and agony of His own death!

God does not record all of the events and conversations that took place during this meal. John, however, offers the most detailed account of the evening (John 13-17). Jesus washed their feet and illustrated the kind of humble servitude that He desires among His people (13:3-20). He told them that one of them would betray Him, and even went so far as to identify Judas to Simon Peter (13:21-26). It must have pained the Lord to see the reaction of the other apostles, as their curiosity degenerated into an argument among themselves about which one would be the greatest in the kingdom (Luke 22:20-30). And as Judas left to complete his treachery, Jesus tried to prepare them for the things that they were about to see. John 14-17 chronicles Christ's final words to His apostles before His death. Their faith was to be tested, inspired, and finally promoted. But on this night, He was concerned - "*Let not your heart be troubled...*" (John 14:1). So Jesus spoke of His leaving, His preparations, His sending of the Spirit, His expectation of their fruitfulness, and His assurance of their success. He completed the instruction with a prayer in John 17—a prayer which culminates in His plea to God that these men, along with all who would believe on Him through their work, "*be one, as You Father, are in Me, and I in You; that they also may be one in Us...*" (John 17:20-23). Their unity would be indispensable when faced with the world's hatred and opposition (verses 11-19), and that same oneness would stand forever as an invincible testimony to the divine nature and authority of Jesus of Nazareth (verses 21-24). The task placed before the apostles was overwhelming. They were fishermen and religious scholars; political rebels and Roman minions; guileless men and sons of thunder; prone to impetuosity and given to ambitious contentions. Yet they were to be one, and thus the example for all of those who would embrace their testimony. And so they were.

Unity among God's children is a challenging goal. In His epistles to first century Christians, God appeals for oneness over and over and over again. Such a resounding repetition should not surprise us, for unity in Christ is a curious achievement. After all, we who come to the Lord bring with us almost innumerable differences. Male and female. Black and white. Rich and poor. Influence and anonymity. Diverse religious backgrounds; distinct national loyalties; various social, educational, political, ideological perspectives. Moral histories that range from pristine to perverted. While Americans tend to view our nation as the world's melting pot, the truth is that God's church long ago secured that distinction. Yet, in Christ, those things that once divided us are to no longer prevail. *"There is neither Jew nor Greek, there is neither slave nor free, there is neither male nor female; for you are all one in Christ Jesus"* (Galatians 3:28). We must recognize that Jesus, in His prayer for unity on the night of His betrayal, was not looking merely at the ambitious arguments of His apostles, but at the overwhelming potential for division among the untold numbers of disciples who would follow. Disciples like us.

> In His epistles to first century Christians, God appeals for oneness over and over and over again.

If we are to appreciate the role of a preacher in the maintaining of unity within a local church, we ought first to appreciate the role of every disciple in such. Preachers are, after all, not exempted from the admonitions and commands of God that involve unity. All too often, it is an ugly unity that permeates local churches. Personalities clash. Trespasses are forgiven but not forgotten. Prejudices arise. Feelings are "sleeve worn" and often injured. Personal failings are exposed. Patience wears thin. Yet people "stay together for the sake of unity." A begrudging togetherness is not unity. God does not call His people to harmony—"a consistent, orderly, or pleasing arrangement of different parts." He calls us to oneness. The question is, "How do we achieve oneness?"

Unity is, first of all, a function of individual devotion to Christ. Paul pleaded with the Corinthian church that *"you all speak the same thing, and that there be no divisions among you, but that you be perfectly joined together in the same mind and in the same judgment"* (1 Corinthians 1:10). The context of that admonition suggests that the Corinthian brethren were being polarized due to divided individual loyalties (verses 11-13). It's not difficult to see how a church might be torn apart when people offer their allegiance to various teachers. Paul's solution to the problem was that they remember that "*of Him (God) you are in Christ Jesus*" (1 Corinthians 1:30) and that they belonged to God (1 Corinthians 3:9f). When we are concerned first and foremost— or perhaps more appropriately singularly and solely—with pleasing God, then and only then will unity be possible among disciples. After all, such was the basis of the unity between Christ and the Father. In the prayer of John 17:20f, Jesus asks that His followers be one, "*as You, Father, are in Me, and I in You.*" That singular mind that united Jesus with His Father was His consistent determination to do the will of the Father (John 4:34; 5:30; 6:38f; 7:16,28f; 8:28f; 9:4). If my goal is to please God, and your goal is to please God, then unity among us is all but guaranteed. But if our loyalties are found anywhere else, division is unavoidable.

In Galatians 3:26f, Paul reminded those divided brethren that they had all "*put on Christ*" and that such mutual devotion had changed them. They were no longer different. They were all one, because they were all now like Christ. The same argument is offered as the basis of a variety of "*one another*" instructions in Colossians 3:9-16. We have "*put on the new man who is renewed in knowledge according to the image of Him who created him*" (verse 10), and every earthly distinction has been dissolved in our mutual acknowledgment of Jesus as Lord (verse 11). Again, if I have "*put on Christ*" and you have "*put on Christ,*" then unity is insured.

Secondly, unity is a function of personal devotion to Christ's Word. Jesus consistently equated discipleship with adherence to His teaching. "*If you love Me, keep My commandments*" (John 14:15). "*If you abide in My word, you are My disciples indeed*" (John 8:31). "*But why do you call me, 'Lord, Lord' and do not do the things which I say?*" (Luke 6:46). It is often the case in the present general religious environment that people "serve Christ" according to personal preference. Many choose a church based upon the programs, worship, or doctrines that they prefer, rather than upon the basis of God's revelation. In such circumstances, unity occurs only when your preferences are the same as my preferences and Christ is dethroned as Lord in favor of ourselves. In Ephesians 4:4f, the "*one body...Spirit...hope...Lord...faith...baptism...God*" are all foundations of unity which have been designated and revealed by God in His Word. They are not subject to whim and opinion. These elements of our service are clearly described for us in the New Testament, and our allegiance to that revelation supplies a basis for our unity. Paul's appeal to the Corinthians that they *"speak the same thing...be perfectly joined together in the same mind and in the same judgment"* (1 Corinthians 1:10) demands a common standard which we can adopt as the basis of our speaking, our mind, and our judgment. If I am following the Word, and you are following the Word, oneness must result. True unity is impossible in the absence of such. When we begin to focus on anything else—our own opinions, preferences, desires, traditions, etc.—unity will flounder.

Thirdly, unity is a function of personal disposition. Oneness demands a common Lord and a common standard, but ultimately oneness demands a common selfless dedication toward the Lord, the standard, and others who are similarly inclined. People may well claim some allegiance to Christ and His Word, but that allegiance is evidenced only in a total submission to both. The "personal devotion" previously noted is demanded by Christ in Matthew 16:24 - *"If anyone desires to come after Me, let him deny himself, and take up his cross, and follow Me."* And the path that Jesus would have us follow calls us to unity with others who are following Him. Given our common Lord and standard, one would think such unity would be natural, yet ultimately it is our attitude toward other disciples that makes unity achievable. Paul admonishes, encourages, instructs, and implores his brethren that they be unified in almost every epistle. He reminds the Romans that we will stand in judgment before God, not before other Christians (Romans 14-15). He scolded the Corinthians for their divided loyalties (1 Corinthians 1-3), warned them about the divisive egoism of their own liberty (1 Corinthians 8-10), and encouraged them to edify one another as a part of one body (1 Corinthians 12-14). He told the Galatians to *"through love serve one another"* rather than suffering the destruction of their own contentions (Galatians 5:13-15f). The Ephesian letter revolves around our common adoption in the family of God, where the union of Jew and Gentile stands as testimony of God's wisdom (Ephesians 1-3). Concluding that thought, Paul begs them to walk *"with lowliness and gentleness, with longsuffering, bearing with one another in love, endeavoring to keep the unity of the Spirit in the bond of peace"* (Ephesians 4:2-3). He directed the Colossians toward *"one another"* obligations which grow out of *"new man"* allegiances (Colossians 3:1-16f). His directives to the

Philippians are perhaps the most instructive for those devoted to unity. "...*fulfill my joy by being likeminded, having the same love, being of one accord, of one mind. Let nothing be done through selfish ambition or conceit, but in lowliness of mind let each esteem others better than himself. Let each of you look out not only for his own interests, but also for the interests of others. Let this mind be in you which also was in Christ Jesus...He humbled Himself...*" (Philippians 2:1-8). A group of disciples who serve Christ in devotion to His Word <u>with selfless, humble,</u> and sacrificial minds will consistently be unified. His will is going to be their will. His goals will be their goals. His character will be their character. His attitude will be their attitude. They cannot but be one. However disunity and division are inevitable when self intervenes. Division always—always—begins with "I." When my opinions, wants, preferences, feelings, ambitions, jealousies, prejudices, ego, or any other selfish concerns begin to drive my "service," then I will dissolve any possible unity with other Christians.

> Frequently we simply forget that faith in Christ demands patience or self-control, poverty of spirit or meekness, forgiveness or self-sacrifice, mercy or kindness.

No one is exempted from these principles. Yet disciples sometimes forget who we are, and Who we serve. Unity is all too often sacrificed when we are faced with circumstances that try the practical expressions of our faith. Occasionally, perhaps, a Christian will completely lose his/her confidence in God due to some life crisis. But more frequently we simply forget that faith in Christ demands patience or self-control, poverty of spirit or meekness, forgiveness or self-sacrifice, mercy or kindness. Some problem arises that affects us personally—a moral failure, a doctrinal issue, a wrongdoing—and we retain our conviction that God is and that He rewards His people and that Christ died on the cross for our sins and that we can be forgiven. But we forget what those truths demand of us. We fail to be godly. And we fail of oneness.

I suspect that every individual disciple and every local congregation has some experience with such a circumstance. Who knows how many local churches exist in this country alone, as a result of disciples who failed at unity in times of difficulty. Rather than conform to humble godliness, we are prone to "go worship elsewhere," even if "elsewhere" doesn't yet exist. Unity is tough. It demands that we face one another, swallow our pride, admit our mistakes, listen to others, forgive and receive forgiveness, deny ourselves, focus on others. Honestly, it is often easier on us just to go and "start a new work." Easier, but not right. How can we be one when Christians in one congregation will not recognize or worship with Christians in another? Do we really believe that such disunity will exist in heaven?

Those who serve God's people in positions of leadership bear a great responsibility when it comes to unity because leadership—whether in some designated capacity (overseers, deacons, teachers, preachers), or whether in some "unofficial" role (a man/woman of repute, talent, experience, age, etc.) - exerts influence. Peter called for elders to be *examples to the flock* (1 Peter 5:3). Paul demanded of Timothy that he be *an example to the believers* (1 Timothy 4:12). Older men and older women are reminded of the import of their character and example in Titus 2:1-5. Those who lead must be ever aware of the impact of their activities, attitudes, reactions, and judgments. Yet, unfortunately, division often reigns because those who lead God's people lead them away from each other. And whether or not it should be so, it is the voices of preachers that often rise above the fray, and herald the dissension.

Preachers, due to the nature of their work, possess the capacity for great good, and for great evil. Their job is to proclaim the gospel (2 Timothy 2:2; 4:1f), and such proclamation lends itself to the possibility of great influence. As teachers of the Word, preachers are often consulted for their knowledge or confided in because of their experience. They become objects of affection as those who lead people to the gospel, and the variety of personalities and abilities and styles that distinguish them sometime results in preferences and even allegiances. Is that not what Paul describes in Corinth in 1 Corinthians 1:10f? It is not particularly difficult to see how the "pastor system" in modern denominationalism arose, for people at times pedestalize their ministers, and ministers at times accept and even promote such. So much influence can be a heady temptation toward self-importance, and all that is necessary for problems to arise is a simple objection, criticism, or even disagreement. Suddenly, the preacher's ego becomes threatened and the process of self-defense, self-promotion, and the systematic decimation of the "enemy" begins. Sermons begin to revolve around the issue at hand. Private conversations are salted with innuendo and suggestion. People are encouraged to side with one man and against another. "The Issue" becomes a litmus test of allegiance, and the true work of preaching the gospel, building up the body of Christ, and seeking the lost is somewhere misplaced in the congregational civil war.

Shame on us, when we would divide the body of Christ over personal pride.

Those of us who preach need to be reminded of our place, much as Jesus reminded James and John when they wanted to destroy a Samaritan village - "*You do not know what manner of spirit you are of*" (Luke 9:55). It would be naive to ignore the potential influence that we exert as preachers and teachers, but it is egregious when we forget who we are. Our work is to save souls—to promote Jesus Christ as Savior and Lord. We must maintain, at all times, an honest and singular devotion to that goal. We are not promoting self, no matter how impressed we may be with our own opinions, preferences, or judgments. In fact, when we become impressed with such things, we have failed in the very discipleship that we proclaim. Preachers are amenable to the demands of the beatitudes (Matthew 5:3-12). We are disciples who must manifest humility, service, self-sacrifice (Matthew 20:25-28). We are obligated to "*add to your faith*" virtue, knowledge, self-control, perseverance, godliness, brotherly kindness, and love" (2 Peter 1:5f). We are exempt from no demands regarding discipleship, and are in fact instructed to be examples "*in word, in conduct, in love, in spirit, in faith, in purity*" (1 Timothy 4:12). Our aim is to serve God's people, and to do so, God's people must come before self, no matter the attack, the criticism, the problem. "*Let this mind be in you which was also in Christ Jesus...*" (Philippians 2:5f) ought to be hand-written and sitting on the desk of every man who stands before others to proclaim the good news of salvation, and at the end of the day, no matter how many sermons we've preached, no matter how many souls have been saved, no matter how much good has been done - "*when you have done all those things which you are commanded, say, we are unprofitable servants. We have done what was our duty to do*" (Luke 17:10). Paul reminded us that the power is in God's Word (Romans 1:16; 1 Corinthians 3:5f), not in ourselves.

Do such admonitions to humble service demand compromise and concession? No. And yes. As heralds of God's Word, we cannot fail to defend such against attack, perversion, misrepresentation, or abuse. While elders are assigned that role in local churches (Titus 1:9), so are evangelists (Titus 1:10-13; 1 Timothy1:3f; 4:1f; 6:11f; 2 Timothy 4:1f). We must be willing to engage in conflict - "*casting down arguments and every high thing that exalts itself against the knowledge of God*" (2 Corinthians 10:5), and if the declaration of truth results in division, so be it. The Lord promised such (Matthew 10:34f). But we must also remember that spiritual warfare is no call to personal dominion. Our attitude must ever be humble, merciful, caring, godly. The "*servant of the Lord*" in 2 Timothy 2:24 is the evangelist in his work. And where issues revolve around opinion, preference, personality, or discrepancies in maturity, preachers ought to be first to concede our own liberty, for such is the demand of mature leadership and godly influence (1 Corinthians 8:13; 9:19-23; 10:29-33). If division is to take place, let it be because of Truth, not because of our disposition.

James warns us all concerning the particular challenges that are borne by those who teach. He cautions those whose ambitions drive them to such public service, "*knowing that we will receive a stricter judgment*" (James 3:1). The warnings about the tongue are offered to teachers who use theirs so frequently, but it is the spirit of "*envy and self-seeking*" (verse 14) that James is decrying. It is a sad reality that people sometimes disguise personal ambition behind the facade of gospel proclamation. That simple warning ought to prompt those who preach to ask themselves continually, "Who am I pleasing?"

Unity within a local congregation is a challenge. So many distinctions must be subdued so that Christ is what permeates each individual, and thus the collectivity. Oneness is possible and powerful when accomplished (John 17:21f). And though Jesus prayed for such, He is not offering so much a wish, as a command. If we are to be united to Him, we have no choice but to pursue unity with one another. Single-minded devotion to Christ and to His Word will produce such. Such devotion begins with the attitude and aim of each individual - "*with all lowliness and gentleness, with longsuffering, bearing with one another in love, endeavoring to keep the unity of the Spirit in the bond of peace*" (Ephesians 4:2-3). That includes those who reside behind the preacher's door.

The Preacher's Friends
Ken Weliever

"It's lonely at the top" says Kevin Kearns, President of Kearns Advantage, a leadership coaching company. "While a cliche', there is a lot of truth in that statement." A leader has few people with whom he can really open up and be transparent. This is especially true for men. Studies have shown that women have more friends than men. Also women define friendship differently. British sociologist Marion Crawford found that, by an overwhelming margin, women described a friend in terms of "trust" and "confidentiality," while men looked at friendship as revolving around activities. Most men are not as apt to share their feelings or reveal their problems to another man

Preachers are uniquely affected by this "lonely at the top" syndrome. We are in a position of leadership. Most of us are like other men with an aversion to talking about our feelings or personal problems. We would rather hang out with our friends to hunt, fish, or watch sporting events! We are in a situation where people come to us for advice, counsel, and spiritual direction, believing we are unlike them, or that we have no problems. Or that we are above temptation. The common impression may be that we have our spiritual life all together. After all, we're preachers!

> We are in a situation where people come to us for advice, counsel, and spiritual direction, believing we are unlike them, or that we have no problems.

When it comes to having someone to confide in, generally there are few (we think), if any with whom we feel comfortable in discussing a problem, confessing some sin, or admitting a reoccurring temptation. We may also feel distrusting of some preachers who may have violated confidences, or fear their disfavor. The easy thing to do is to withdraw, isolate ourselves, and suffer in silence.

So, what's a preacher to do?

Admit We Need Friends

The wise man observed, "Ointment and perfume delight the heart, and the sweetness of a man's friend gives delight by hearty counsel. Do not forsake your own friend or your father's friend," (Proverbs 27:9-10). Keil and Delitzsch observe how the ancients perfumed with dry aromas and the sprinkling of liquid aromas "as a mark of honor toward guests and a means of promoting joyful social fellowship." In the same way friends provide delight. Give pleasure. Offer counsel. Furnish joy. We preachers need the delight of such friends.

> If Jesus spent special time with His friends, praying, sharing His passion and confiding in them, how much more do we need true friends?

Jesus valued friendships. He spent more time with His chosen twelve than He did the multitudes. We often see Him getting away from the crowds with His friends for a period of rest and reflection. Among them He had an inner circle—Peter, James, and John who was identified as "the disciple whom Jesus loved" (John 21:20). Think about this. If Jesus spent special time with His friends, praying, sharing His passion and confiding in them, how much more do we need true friends?

Furthermore, much of Jesus' teaching had to do with friendship and fellowship. The "golden rule" (Matthew 7:12), "the second great commandment" (Matthew 22:37), and the "new commandment" (John 13:33-35) all speak to the issue of relationships. Jesus meant for us to share life together. To find fulfillment in a community of believers who share each other's sorrows, bear each other's burdens, and care for each other's hurts. We must remember that this is not just for the folks we preach to...it's for you and me. We need each other. We need friends.

What Friends can Do for Each Other

The necessity of our friendships is affirmed by the value they add to our lives. As preachers we will have those who want to hold us "at arm's length," look for the flaw in our lives, be suspicious of our motives, or seek our friendship as a "status symbol." So, we must look for real friends. True

Friends. Loyal friends. These kinds of friends are priceless. They are the kind of whom the Preacher speaks in Ecclesiastes 4:9-12.

> *Two are better than one,*
> *Because they have a good reward for their labor.*
> *For if they fall, one will lift up his companion.*
> *But woe to him who is alone when he falls,*
> *For he has no one to help him up.*
> *Again, if two lie down together, they will keep warm;*
> *But how can one be warm alone?*
> *Though one may be overpowered by another, two can withstand him.*
> *And a threefold cord is not quickly broken.*
> *NKJV*

Notice what the wise man says about the value of a real friend.

(1) A Real Friend Helps You when You're Down (verse 10).

How can you tell the difference between friends and acquaintances? That's easy. Just get into trouble and see who is still around! They are available day or night. When it's convenient or inconvenient. Yes, "A friend loves at all times, and a brother is born for adversity" (Proverbs 17:17).

There have been times in my life when I experienced setbacks in the local work or personal challengers that discouraged me and I had the blessing of friends who were older and more experienced to offer wise advice. Without sharing the discouraging details, I remember a lunch several years with Raymond Harris and Aude McKee. These friends were there for me when I needed them. They offered their compassion, care, and counsel. I will never forget it.

(2) A Real Friend Provides Emotional or Physical Warmth in a Cold World (verse 11).

Sometimes we take a passage so literally that we miss the point. This is not just about keeping someone warm physically. It applies emotionally. There are situations that leave our emotional gas gauge on empty. This is a time we need friends to provide warmth, comfort, and consolation.

In 1975 when my brother was tragically killed in an automobile accident, I was devastated. After the funeral with a one week break, I had to return to the pulpit. It was hard. But the brethren in Palmetto, Florida, provided emotional support. I will always be indebted to their many acts of kindness and compassion when I was hurting and emotionally drained.

> **I will always be indebted to many acts of kindness and compassion when I was hurting and emotionally drained.**

(3) A Real Friend will Fight to Protect You (verse 12).

That passage was written based on the military strategy of the ancient world. Almost all combat was hand to hand. Soldiers went into battle with a partner, someone who could be counted on and trusted. They stood back to back and fought any enemy that came from the side. True friends never stab you in the back, but they guard your back. A real friend will protect your reputation.

A loyal friend will stand up for you. A faithful friend will not allow someone else to take advantage of you.

(4) A Real Friend is Committed to Helping You Grow.

Another trait of a friend is found in Proverbs 27:17. "*As iron sharpens iron, a friend sharpens a friend.*" True friends want to see their friends improve, grow, and get better. A person who is jealous or resentful of your growth is not a true friend. Author John Maxwell uses the expression "bringing something to the table" as it applies to relationships. What value are your friends adding to your life? Are they helping you? Or hurting you? Do they encourage your growth? Or delight in your decline? Choose friends that will help you grow as a preacher.

As a young preacher, I was blessed to have older friends like Paul Andrews. Once when I was facing the daunting task of preaching on the work and qualities of elders, Paul shared some material that really helped me. I still use many of the ideas that he contributed to my knowledge base as a young preacher. The times I spent with men like Robert Jackson, Aude McKee, and James P. Miller helped me grow as a preacher.

Of course, it is fair for each of us to ask ourselves, "What value am I adding to my friendships? What ideas am I sharing? What help am I providing? What resources am I offering? Am I a reservoir or a river?"

> The times I spent with men like Robert Jackson, Aude McKee, and James P. Miller helped me grow as a preacher.

The One Thing You Need

When we are struggling, whether it is with finances, relationships, temptations, family or church problems there is one thing that we absolutely need: **ENCOURAGEMENT!** Preachers need friends who will encourage instead of discourage, edify instead of destroy, and energize instead of depress. We all know people who you don't dare talk to about your problems because they will make you feel worse, or they immediately want to tell you how your problems are nothing compared to their problems!

There is an old adage that contains some element of truth: Don't tell anyone about your problems because 50% of people don't care and the other 50% are glad you have them! While I think that is a slight exaggeration, it does illustrate that we need to be selective in whom we confide. Look for those with the gift of encouragement.

Dr. David Jeremiah wrote in his fine book "The Power of Encouragement": *"The ministry of encouragement is like a car that comes alongside ours and gives us a jump start. The strength of the operative car is transferred into the weak battery, and the inoperative car is rejuvenated to action. When we see people who are discouraged, saddened by the hardships of life, or simply tired of the Christian path of obedience, we need to come alongside and give them a spiritual jump start. As Christ and other members of the Body of Christ strengthen us, we can strengthen each other."* What a great analogy! Look for friends with emotional and spiritual batteries that are fully charged. Search out people with the ability and gift to give you a "jump start."

Encouragement is the need of our day. As preachers we spend much of our time encouraging others. Ironically such work can be emotionally draining, causing us to need encouragement from others. Have you ever felt like David when he lamented, "No one cares for my soul"? (Psalm 142:4). There is no shame in feeling discouraged, disheartened and dismayed. David did. We need to be transparent enough to admit there are times when we require encouragement.

> **Be sensitive to your fellow workers in the Lord and use opportunities to lift them up when they are down.**

The very essence of the "one another" commands is rooted in the concept of encouragement. Paul admonished, "*Therefore encourage one another and build each other up, just as in fact you are doing*" (1 Thessalonians 5:11). In times of death, the apostle said, "encourage each other" (1 Thessalonians 4:18). Romans 12:6 speaks of using our different gifts and in verse 8 Paul wrote "*if it is encouraging, let us encourage.*" Look for those with the gift of encouragement. Be sensitive to your fellow workers in the Lord and use opportunities to lift them up when they are down.

There are various ways in which we can give and receive encouragement. Consider these.

(1) By what we sense. Job's three friends came to encourage him in time of deep despair. They didn't end up being much of an encouragement, but they did do something right in the beginning—they came and sat with him for seven days and said nothing! We may receive encouragement from someone who "is there for us." Often we may find ourselves on the giving end of one seeking encouragement and don't know what to say. Sometimes all we need to do is sit there and be with them.

(2) By what we see. Many of the New Testament letters were written to encourage brethren. We can look into God's wonderful word and see many things that encourage us (Psalm 119:18), but we can be strengthened by the notes of encouragement we receive from others. I save notes. I call it my "good file." Occasionally I take them out and read some things that people have written to me through the years. I am always encouraged when I do. The lesson here is two fold: (1) Look for encouragement in what you see from others. (2) Be a person who takes the time to write words of encouragement to fellow preachers. Your words may be read weeks, months, or even years later.

(3) By what we hear. The wise man observed, *"Anxiety in the heart of a man weighs it down, but a good word makes it glad"* (Proverbs 12:25, NAS). He also wrote, *"Pleasant words are a honeycomb, sweet to the soul and healing to the bones"* (Proverbs 16:24, NIV). When you are disheartened, seek the company of someone who has a good word, a kind word, a healing and helping word. It will make your heart glad.

(4) By what we feel. We also get encouragement from what we feel when others embrace us. The wise man said, "there is a time to embrace" (Ecclesiastes 3:5). Friends can provide a warm hug, handshake, or pat on the back that makes us feel better. Have you ever noticed how many times Jesus used the "power of touch" in interacting with people? Not just in a miraculous way, but in a way that said to lepers, blind people and hurting people, **"I care about you."** They were encouraged when the Lord touched them.

Encouragement may take the form of sympathy, empathy, instruction, admonition, or even a loving and kind reproof. We need all of those things at different seasons of our lives. Let's be willing to receive it when we need it and offer it to our friends in time of need.

Who are the Preacher's Friends?

The preacher is friends with everyone! Yet realism tells us that not everyone can fill our need when we are feeling disheartened, struggling with a problem, or fighting temptation. There are those who can help, but there are those that cannot, and should not.

Do we need to be reminded, fellow preachers, that we should not talk to the sisters in the church (or any other women) about personal marital problems? How many times has that happened, either innocently, ignorantly, or intentionally and a much worse problem ensued? Weak brethren don't need to hear about our problems. New Christians are not a good sounding board regardless of our friendship. Brethren who have a weakness with gossip cannot be trusted with sensitive issues we are facing. Much of this ought to be obvious, but in a moment of helplessness or foolishness, preachers have confided in the wrong people.

Depending on the nature, complexity, and severity of the challenges preachers face, let me recommend some friends.

> **Men that we trust with confidential information who possess knowledge and wisdom can help us with many struggles that are unique to the preacher.**

(1) Fellow Preachers. My co-workers in Christ have been a source of encouragement, enlightenment and strength through the years. Men that we trust with confidential information who possess knowledge and wisdom can help us with many struggles that are unique to the preacher. There are some things that we just can't talk to anyone else about who really understands what we're dealing with. A word of caution is offered here. Our motives must be pure. We must be honestly seeking help, insight and direction. Meeting with other preachers for a gossip session, without any real desire to find a solution is not the answer. Of course, sometimes we just need to talk to "get something off our chest." However, be careful not to abuse your friendship with other preachers just to gripe about real or imagined grievances.

(2) Pastors. The elders are the spiritual shepherds of the flock. They watch for the souls of God's Family—that includes us preachers. I can think of times when I was facing a decision or seeking the best solution to a problem, and of finding the answer from a sensitive Shepherd. Again judgment is needed depending on the nature of the problem, but godly men in whom we have total confidence are capable through years of experience to offer wise counsel.

(3) Brethren. While we are "friends with everyone" most preachers have a close friend or two in the church with whom they are comfortable talking about things. It is not wrong to have 2-3 close friends; even Jesus had his inner circle. Again caution must be exercised not to disclose information that may be harmful to you or the church, but certain brethren, due to the nature of their profession or experience, may well serve as close confidants when we experience certain kinds of challenges.

(4) Your Wife. If you are married, the one to whom you pledged yourself in sickness, health, good times and bad, should be your number one encourager! Don't be too proud to take advice from your wife! She often understands relationships better than you do and can offer excellent guidance.

(5) Professional Counselors. I offer this suggestion with some reservation and qualification. Not all psychotherapy is good. Humanistic counselors may give advice that is at odds with the Bible. Yet there are a number of "Christian counselors" who can help you with family and marital problems, addictions, or financial issues. If we have a problem with our car, we go to a mechanic. If we have a toothache, we call a dentist. If you have a relationship problem or emotional issue, get assistance from someone who is qualified to help.

(6) Books. Groucho Marx once quipped, "Outside of a dog, a book is a man's best friend. Inside of a dog it's too dark to read." Well, books can be good friends. A book can counsel. Warn. Enlighten. Inspire. Reassure. Direct. Don't neglect reading, my preacher friend. I have often found the answer to some challenge I faced or question I was wrestling with from the pages of a good book.

(7) Jesus! Let's don't forget Him. We sing, "What a friend we have in Jesus." It's true. Jesus was and is the friend of sinners (Matthew 11:19). He wants to be our friend. We can go to Him with our sorrows, sin, and shame. Sometimes, we just need to "have a little talk with Jesus."

Preachers Need People

There is an old Barbara Streisand song that says, "people who need people are the luckiest people in the world." God created us for community. Life is about people and relationships. Our success in ministry is dependent upon forging and fostering good relationships. We know that, but it is easy to think that is for everyone else in the church, not us. As preachers, let us work to role model godly relationships, develop friendships, and seek the companionship of those on whom we can rely in good times and bad. What a blessing it is to have "a friend that sticks closer than a brother."

The Preacher's Toys - Technology's Impact on His Work

Edwin Crozier

I can hardly imagine how Paul worked as an evangelist. He had no iPhone, no Internet, no computer software. If he wanted to talk to someone, he actually had to travel to meet them. He could write a letter, but who knew how long it would take to get there. He could read the Law, but he had to go to a synagogue and pull out a scroll (that is, if the local Jews would let him anywhere near the synagogue). He couldn't preach to the masses via the radio or the television. He couldn't record his sermons and pass them on to anyone unless someone who actually knew how to write transcribed what he said and then made copies by hand.

Technology is amazing. We can study more easily than ever before. We have software that puts scholarship at our fingertips. Not to mention if we have a question, the Internet is there with a ready answer. We don't even have to take a trip to the library anymore.

We have more access to more learning than ever before. We can find video, audio, and print media with more study on more topics. If we really like another preacher, we can probably find his sermons online. We can sync our mp3 players to the sermons of a dozen preachers per week. We can download audio books and listen to them in the car. We can "study" while we're driving.

Study materials are getting cheaper than ever before. Don't get me wrong; souped-up Bible programs cost a pretty penny. However, as more and more study materials and books end up online, we can get access to them for a fraction of the cost of the preacher's traditional library (though some of us still prefer the feel of a real book and probably always will). Of course there's always blueletterbible.com or biblegateway.com—free Bible study on the web with all kinds of research tools.

We can place more evangelistic tools in the hands of our brethren than ever before. We can podcast our sermons. We can stream our services online. We can pdf anything and let it be disseminated with the click of a button. Correspondence courses can be put online and automatically graded with little effort from us. With webcams and Skype we can have one-on-one studies with anyone all over the world.

We can connect with others more easily than ever before. We can make a call while we are commuting. We can teleconference. We can search the web on our phones. We can text anyone. If we want to keep up with people, we can connect on Pleonast, Facebook, and Twitter. Not to mention, through these media, we readily learn a side of people they keep hidden in the assemblies, letting us better know what help people need from the Scripture.

We can communicate with our brethren more readily. We don't have to set up phone trees; an e-mail list will do the job. A website can keep the brethren informed on all the upcoming events. With Twitter, we can keep all of our elders, deacons, teachers, group leaders, study groups, or whoever informed with up to the minute information tweeted to their cell phones. Not to mention the yellow pages ad is a thing of the past, a good website with SEO (search engine optimization) can put each of us on the top of someone's search on Google. We don't need big bucks advertising; we can cheaply use social media.

With Google's Web Alerts, we can even quickly learn if there is any social media gossip about us. We can enter our name or the church's name into their alert system and if we end up on the web, we'll know in short order. Just this morning I learned that a bulletin article from the franklinchurchofchrist.com was copied and redistributed on someone else's website through this service.

Then there is PowerPoint. Editorial policy doesn't allow me to name names, but let's face it, not many of us are "that preacher." Our sermons could use a little pizzazz, a bit of zip; okay, they could use some help in the not so memorable places. Never fear, a good PowerPoint presentation can help sink a spoken message into the memories of our audience.

Who can deny that technology is the preacher's friend?

The Dark Side of Technology

However, technology can also be the preacher's enemy. Just as modern technology has given rise to unprecedented help, it has also provided unprecedented danger. Of course, technology has not really presented any new dangers; it has just made some old dangers frighteningly easy. Allow me to share the 10 top dangers I see with modern technology.

> Technology has not really presented any new dangers; it has just made some old dangers frighteningly easy.

Danger #1: Technology can breed materialism and covetousness.

I have an iPhone, but now the iPhone 3GS is out. I just have to have one. Not to mention the computer I bought two years ago is now obsolete. Back then, memory came in gigabytes. I need terabytes. I want to put videos online. I have to have the latest easy to use YouTube ready video camera. If I could only have the latest and greatest planning software/device I would really be streamlined and get some real work done. I probably wouldn't be behind on my deadline with this chapter if I owned better time management software.

Do you see the problem? I want, I want, I want. I hate to bring up the starving preachers in Africa, but some of those brothers would like to eat every day, and I'm going in debt so I can surf the web on my phone anywhere, anytime.

No doubt, these technologies aren't wrong. If you can afford them, enjoy them. However, let's face it; our salaries aren't set for endless technological pursuit. At some point we have to develop some technological contentment.

Danger #2: Technology can steal our time.

Facebook is awesome. We can connect with people from our entire lives. I've talked with high school and college friends I otherwise would never have seen again. I have been able to develop relationships with Christians from gospel meetings that I would have simply forgotten. I think I'm being a positive influence on folks I otherwise would never even know. However, when I first got on Facebook, I spent half my time keeping up on those relationships without even realizing it. Then there were the days at the office when I would complete a project and say, "I'll just take a ten-minute break and check Facebook." An hour later I was saying, "Just five more minutes." Three or four breaks like that in a day and at the end of the week I was wondering why my sermons weren't done.

> Three or four breaks like that in a day and at the end of the week I was wondering why my sermons weren't done.

Then there are the discussion lists and online groups discussing Bible issues. I don't know how many Bible studies encouraging the brethren in my own congregation I could have had with the time I wasted arguing on Pleonast two years ago. We convince ourselves it is part of our work because it is Bible discussion. But the work we are actually supported to do suffers.

Sadly, sometimes just plain old good stuff takes up too much of our time. Many good preachers are putting their sermons online or sending daily devotionals via e-mail, Facebook, or blogs. If I read everything that comes up in my RSS feed, my e-mail, or my Facebook notes, it would take all day, every day. We can't read or listen to it all. We'll have to pick and choose and sacrifice some of it.

Danger #3: Technology provides temptations to immorality.

Not a week goes by that my Twitter account is not followed by someone who wants me to check out their get rich quick scheme, their online gambling, their dating service, or their pornography. One time, someone who followed me had a tweet that looked like the start of an article on the present recession. I clicked the link to read the rest of the article; it took me to a porn site. This morning I checked Facebook and there was an ad offering to tell me which women had been Googling my name alongside a picture of a lustful woman leaning against her bed. No matter how strong you are, these gimmicks can sucker punch you.

Danger #4: Technology can cause us to isolate and disconnect from people.

We are deceived into believing that we are more connected than ever because of technology. However, these connections are not real. There is no eye contact, no physical touch. There is nothing of the actual intimacy (non-sexual) that we need to thrive emotionally. Instead of actually dealing with issues face-to-face, we sometimes destroy relationships with the click of a button. We feel more comfortable because we don't have to deal with our emotions as we look someone in the eye, but that is part of mature relationships.

Texting someone the night before their big surgery is not the connection and support they need. Giving counsel in an online support group for those who have lost loved ones is not the same as weeping with those who weep. Sending an e-mail of congratulations is not the best way of rejoicing with those who rejoice. Hospitality is not forwarding someone an electronic gift card to a local restaurant. We need real connection and so do the people we teach and serve.

Because of the disconnect that comes with technology, we can destroy relationships by typing something in ways we would never speak if we were actually looking in someone's eyes.

Finally, because of the disconnect that comes with technology, we can destroy relationships by typing something in ways we would never speak if we were actually looking in someone's eyes. Lack of facial expression, body language, and tone of voice can take even the most innocent of conversations and allow them to kill a relationship. I don't know how many posts in online discussions I wish I could take back. I deleted some of them, but the damage was already done. It is just too easy to type a knee-jerk reaction and hit "send" before thinking it through.

Danger #5: Technology can lead to laziness.

Obviously there is the mental laziness that comes with knowing a machine can do our work for us. The fact is, I have almost completely forgotten my multiplication tables because I have a calculator. But my job isn't accounting, so who cares about that? What really concerns me is how easy it is to avoid personal study all week long and then Google a good sermon on Saturday. Don't get me wrong; we don't need to reinvent the wheel every week. However, just as no Christian can spiritually live off someone else's study, neither can a preacher survive off someone else's work.

Another form of laziness is finding a quote online but not checking its original context to make sure you are using it correctly. Or worse, finding a quote online and not checking to make sure the person actually said it (Google "Shane Fitzgerald Maurice Jarre" to find a host of stories about this problem).

Danger #6: Technology can lead to plagiarism.

Speaking of stealing, I'm sorry, Googling sermons...

Of course, most of us preachers who put our lessons on the web want them to be used. We aren't necessarily looking for credit, but it is bad form to present someone else's work as your own. However, I'm really less concerned with this than I am about just down home, garden-variety plagiarism. Preachers can find all kinds of information online and add it into their articles and sermons. There is nothing wrong with that; we just need to give proper credit. When we provide statistics and claims, we need to give a reference so our readers and hearers can check our facts. Of course, this doesn't have to be based in technology. Many a preacher (including me) has read a good book and presented a sermon as if he had just been studying the Bible and come up with that neat alliterative sermon all on his own. Don't be so caught up in wanting to look good to your audience that you deceive them. (Also, be careful, because sometimes those authors really stretch the integrity of a text just to get their point to start with a "P".)

Danger #7: Technology can lead us to propagate bad information.

The Internet is not peer reviewed. It is not monitored for accuracy. It is good because in some ways we might find out some truths that would otherwise be kept from us. However, we must understand that just because something is on the Internet doesn't make it so. We need to cross-reference and cross check whatever we learn there before we put it in our sermons, articles, or e-mails.

Oh yes, and please, don't pass along another e-mail that says, "I don't know if this is true, but just in case…"

Danger #8: Technology can lead to gossip and slander.

This is tied with the last danger. When we pass on bad information about people, we are gossiping and slandering. That is true even if it is about the presidential candidate we just can't stand. It's especially true if we are passing on information about another preacher, elder, Christian. Even if what we are passing on is true, it might still be slander and gossip. Will the information cause others to think ill of someone? That's gossip.

Danger #9: Technology can lead us to think more highly of ourselves than we ought.

Some preachers have spent years learning the original languages, the historical backgrounds, the geographical nuances of the Scriptures. These can sometimes speak from a position of authority about these topics. The rest of us have a good Bible program with a Strong's reference system and an easy to use lexicon. We can grasp just enough of these more specialized skills to make us dangerous. If we are not careful, we begin to think we are more expert than we really are and then preach lessons that, to students of the Greek language would sound a lot like us explaining that a butterfly is an airborne dairy product.

Danger #10: Technology can lead us to be downright annoying.

Don't add someone to your bulletin e-mail list unless they ask. If someone didn't accept your invitation to be a fan of your congregation or your devotional material on Facebook, don't keep badgering them with invitations, and please, no matter how important you think the issue is, stop forwarding e-mails that tell us we don't love Jesus if we don't forward it to 10 other people.

Implementing Some Safeguards

Can we navigate the dangerous rapids of technology while still being able to use it wisely? Here are five safeguards I believe will help.

Safeguard #1: Remember what your job really is.

"I charge you in the presence of God and of Christ Jesus, who is to judge the living and the dead, and by his appearing and his kingdom: preach the word; be ready in season and out of season; reprove, rebuke, and exhort, with complete patience and teaching" (2 Timothy 4:1-2). This job takes work. Technology does not provide shortcuts to the real work of this job. You are working with a congregation, not the universal church. Your job is to reach lost souls, but to do so with gentleness and care. "The Lord's servant must not be quarrelsome but kind to everyone, able to teach, patiently enduring evil, correcting his opponents with gentleness" (2 Timothy 2:24-25).

Safeguard #2: Make personal study a priority.

Read Psalm 119 and recognize the benefits of God's Word. These are benefits of God's Word, not someone else's podcast about God's Word. We need to spend time in God's Word just to spend time in God's Word. Don't get caught up in the rat race of producing sermons, articles, and classes. That will eventually lead to the shortcuts of Googling and co-opting someone else's work. Study simply to study. Develop a schedule and a plan. You might be amazed at how many sermons you really can come up with on your own when you are studying just to study and not simply trying to make sure you have a sermon for Sunday.

Safeguard #3: Plan real connections with real people.

The early Christians spent time together outside of the assemblies (Acts 2:46-47). Develop a plan to spend real time with real people. Don't settle for the virtual connection of cyberspace. Have people over. Visit the sick. Meet for lunch or coffee. You need to do something with real people outside of the assemblies every week.

> Don't settle for the virtual connection of cyberspace. Have people over. Visit the sick. Meet for lunch or coffee.

Safeguard #4: Keep records and track your time and money.

Ephesians 5:15-16 tells us to make the most of our time. We could say the same thing for our money. Next week keep a record of everything you do. You may be surprised at how much non-productive time you spend surfing the web, chatting on the phone, or answering non-essential e-mails. Take a month and track your money. Where is it going? Is technology destroying your stewardship? After tracking and getting a good idea of where these things are going, start developing plans and budgets to make the most of them. If you don't learn to control your time and money, they'll control you.

Safeguard #5: Be accountable to someone else.

Ecclesiastes 2:9-12 says two are better than one. Jesus always sent the apostles out by twos. Paul always travelled with others. Don't deal with this on your own. Get accountability software on your computer. Share your plans and goals with someone else who has permission to ask you how you are doing. Let your shepherds know how you are working. Let them actually shepherd you, not just be your bosses.

Conclusion

Technology is a wonderful thing and I look forward to seeing how future advances benefit us in our work. However, with each advance will come the accompanying potential for abuse. Let's work together to walk the narrow way as we enjoy the latest and greatest that man invents.

The Preacher as a Husband
Curtis Pope

As far back as I can remember, I have always wanted to preach the gospel. Fortunately, during most of my teenage years I was blessed to worship with brethren who had no "full-time preacher" and who loved me and were patient enough with me to listen, even when I did not have much to say, therefore giving me more pulpit experience than many my age. I preached my first sermon at thirteen; was placed on the preaching rotation by fourteen; did regular appointment preaching by seventeen; and was preaching every Sunday for congregations as "their preacher" by the time I was nineteen.

Learning in the "School of Hard Knocks" as the curriculum above describes, can be brutal with a very high attrition rate. However, such an education can have a significant and unique value. I was blessed to have a mother and father who taught me to love the Lord, my Dad even preaching full-time until I was in Junior High, a father-in-law who always looked at the scriptures with amazingly independent thought, a grandfather who preached most Sundays of his life while working with his hands all week, wonderful teachers (who would later become colleagues) at Florida College who became my mentors, and many other evangelists whose sermons, words of encouragement, and whose interest in me and my work motivated me more than they will ever know, and a supportive, godly wife without whom none of my teaching or preaching would have been possible.

Over the years I have also been given a lot of advice concerning how I could become a better preacher. One of the best pieces of advice I was ever given was this: in order to be a successful evangelist I had to "know the Book" (i.e. the Bible) and I also had to "know men" (i.e. people). Throughout my life I have seen preachers become ineffective because they failed in their understanding of one or both of these subjects. For example, I have seen some men who fit in well with all groups of people, but spiritually starved their brethren with shallow sermons. I have also seen others who locked themselves away in their offices, and in doing so seemed to develop no people skills, or perhaps lose the ones they once had.

As valid as the truism, "know the Book and know men!" has proven to be over the years, several years ago I began to think of it as not completely inclusive of the preacher's duty and training. Several preachers I have run into over the years have been great students of the Word, with strong people skills, but who have lost their passion for both the Word and the souls of lost people. With this in mind, I began to adjust the advice given to me by advising those even younger than myself to "Love the Word, and love Men" to indicate the passionate persistence required of a faithful minister of God's Word.

Recently, however, in looking back over forty-one years of preaching, I have been forced to look back over the lives of men whose lives were spent in the Word and whose love for souls seemed apparent, but whose family lives were such a mess that it was difficult for them to continue as evangelists at one place for any great length of time. The reason for their failure was simple: their wives, or the way they treated their wives, served as an impediment to their work in the Kingdom of God. Sadly, I have even heard of a few men who had no observable skills whatsoever, continuing in local works because everyone loved and respected the preacher's wife. This obvious but disturbing exception to my maxim, and the invitation to write this chapter, have challenged me to explore this often unconsidered work of the preacher as a husband. I intend to do this from a perspective that is both biblical and hopefully practical. I hope to prove from both the Scriptures and common sense that, "Loving God, men, and your wife (if you have one)" sums up fairly well the work of a preacher and provides us all worthy goals to pursue as Christians and as evangelists.

The Marital Status of Preachers

The Bible really has very little to say about preachers marrying or their wives. Simon Peter's wife is mentioned when Jesus heals her mother of a fever (Matthew 8:14-15; Mark 1:29-31; Luke 4:38-39). It is implied that Philip the Evangelist was married in Acts 21:8-9 by mentioning his four virgin daughters that were prophetesses. In defending his apostleship, Paul mentions the wives of the apostles, especially Cephas (Peter), and the Lord's brothers. He mentions this to answer the argument, apparently made against him by his enemies, that he and Barnabas did not accept support from the Corinthian church because they knew they had no right to it as false apostles, and therefore they could not afford to be married in their impoverished condition (1 Corinthians 9: 5-6). In spite of so few verses discussing the marriage of preachers, it does seem clear that apostles, prophets, elders, and preachers were allowed to marry according to the New Testament pattern.

I do believe that it is important to note, however, that two of the most powerful preachers of the New Testament, Jesus and Paul, were unmarried and that likewise, preachers today are under no obligation to marry. In fact, in light of "the present distress" Paul recommended unmarried chastity (1 Corinthians 7:1, 7-8, 26-27). Often I am afraid that in our asserting the rights and benefits of preachers marrying, we do not present this option to our young people as a legitimate alternative for spiritual service. Single men can get by on less support, they can move to places where they are needed which may not be conducive to rearing a family, and they may also move to the religious frontiers of Christianity where they can speak out even more boldly than they could if they knew they were endangering their families. I knew a young man back in the mid-70's who preached and smuggled Bibles into the Soviet Union. The danger of his work made him determine not to marry so his family could never be used as leverage against him by the totalitarian government. In 1 Corinthians 7:28 and 32-34, Paul points out just such troubles and conflicted interests of the one who is married and engaged in gospel work. He describes this not in terms of sin, but simply in terms of the practicalities of life. May God give us men with this spirit "of power and love and discipline" (2 Timothy 1:7).

In spite of Paul's recommendation, however, he does recognize that the single life is not the ideal situation for most people. You can tell Paul is no hopeless romantic when after recommending celibacy, he concedes marriage as the best way to avoid fornication (1 Corinthians 7:2) and admits that "it is better to marry than to burn" (1 Corinthians 7:9). I do not believe that he is even putting marriage in an inferior spiritual position, but simply pointing out some of its disadvantages in the light of difficulties he articulates in the rest of the chapter. All in all, his view would seem to harmonize with that of the Hebrew writer (if it was not Paul himself) who advocated that "marriage be held in honor among all, and let the marriage bed be undefiled;" (Hebrews 13:4).

The Marital Responsibilities of Preachers

> I will even go so far as to say that if your wife cannot feel good about a move that you want to make, DO NOT GO!

The greatest responsibility of a Christian is to "love the Lord your God with all your heart, and with all your soul, and with all your strength, and with all your mind" (Luke 10:27). As we have seen above, if one can show this kind of love and obedience while remaining content, chaste, and single, such a life is pleasing to God. I can think of no reason why this would not apply to a preacher as well. Often brethren want a married man or someone with children, but they must understand that if an evangelist is mature and otherwise qualified, their preferences are not based on Scripture but simply on human opinion. If a minister does decide to marry, however, he must understand that other than loving and serving God, pleasing his wife should be his greatest goal and desire. This may mean he cannot preach everywhere he would like. It may even mean that he cannot preach at all.

A godly man does not have to preach full-time to be pleasing to God, but if he does, he has to be "diligent" in his efforts (2 Timothy 2:15). In spite of the wonderful comfort it is to have a spiritual partner, confidant, and true helper in their work, a gospel preacher does not have to have a wife. But if he does, the physical, emotional, and spiritual needs of his spouse must be met first (1 Corinthians 7:2-3, 32-33) and may even preclude some works the husband might think fruitful. I will even go so far as to say that if your wife cannot feel good about a move that you want to make, DO NOT GO!

Finally, although it is only slightly related to this lesson, the same could be said for your children. Gospel preachers do not have to have children, but if they do, their teaching and welfare must take priority over one's work as an evangelist (Ephesians 6:4; Colossians 3:21). Many preachers have learned this tragic lesson the hard way as they have immersed themselves in foreign work, preaching, or Bible teaching only to find out too late that in saving others they lost their spouse or their children. This is especially tragic when one considers that gospel preaching is an individual, personal choice that can be taken up or laid down, without blame or sin, several times in the life of a faithful Christian man. On the other hand, being a godly husband or father, while still perhaps a choice, is a responsibility laid down only in your death or that of your wife or child, and which involves those who should be the most precious on earth to us. As important as preaching the gospel is, always make sure we first "keep our own back porch swept."

The Preacher as an Example

Perhaps no passage defines the work of the preacher better than 2 Timothy 4:2, "preach the word, be ready in season and out of season; reprove, rebuke, exhort, with great patience and instruction." Certainly preaching and teaching and the study it takes to prepare for those tasks describe the basic work of an evangelist. As this passage suggests, this involves not simply the preparation of an infinite number of presentations, but sufficient feeding on the Word so that God's servant can be ready both "in season and out of season" to "reprove, rebuke, and exhort" from the fullness of his study of the Scriptures. **As the old country preacher said about his own sermon preparation: "I read myself full, I think myself clear, I pray myself hot, then, I let myself go."** The best preachers are always the ones who truly know the Lord and his Word. Many can give a few speeches, but there is a world of difference between those that are glib and those who speak from the overflow of God's Word that fills their lives.

> Many can give a few speeches, but there is a world of difference between those that are glib and those who speak from the overflow of God's Word.

I believe that this is what the apostle Paul wanted to get across to Timothy in 1 Timothy 4:12, "Let no one look down on your youthfulness, but rather in speech, conduct, love, faith, and purity, show yourself an example of those who believe." In telling Timothy to let "no one look down" on the fact that he was young, Paul was mentioning something not completely within his control. To some extent, part of the older population will always look down on the young, but Paul is telling Timothy to **give no one a reason** to undervalue his work by engaging in youthful indiscretions or foolishness. On the contrary, he wants him to live as a role model to those Christians that he works with in Ephesus in "speech, conduct, love, faith, and purity."

Notice the pattern the Holy Spirit revealed through Paul in these two passages about what is expected of ministers. God's servants must preach the Word, but also to be so full of the Scriptures that we know it well enough to utilize it "in season and out of season." But even beyond that, our teaching should be so engrained in us that our lives become sermons as we put the gospel to work in our everyday lives so we can become "example[s] of those who believe." To my knowledge the Scriptures are silent on Timothy's marital status. If he was a husband, how could he as an evangelist also have been exemplary in his marriage?

Examples in Trying to Understand Their Wives

As was mentioned in the beginning of this chapter, the Bible says very little about preachers and their wives. Therefore, the passages I will use will not be passages that apply solely to marital situations. I will, however, try to use some passages given to married couples in general and make some applications to the relationship a preacher should have with his wife. The first such passage is Peter's instruction to husbands in 1 Peter 3:7a, "You husbands likewise, live with your wives in an understanding way, as with a weaker vessel, since she is a woman." You will notice that the Lord does not demand that we understand our wives, but that we live with them "in an understanding way." Understanding them may be beyond our capabilities, but **trying to understand**, and making sure she is aware of your effort can help marital harmony and communication tremendously. For the observant, I am sure this will be no surprise, but men and women are quite different. Not only are we built differently and plumbed differently, but our brains are also wired quite differently. I do not know if it is a left brain/right brain problem, a whole brain (f)/half brain (m) problem or, even as a few women have told me, *a some brain (f)/no brain (m) issue*. But the fact is men and women, with a few exceptions think, act, and communicate differently than men.

Why the "Judge of all the earth" (Genesis 18:25) would institute marriage as a life-long union with two beings who can barely understand each other has often been a mystery to me. But knowing that "the judgments of the Lord are true; they are righteous altogether" (Psalm 19:9), I trust that the patience we must learn in the process of learning to communicate with someone who thinks differently than ourselves and caring enough to try, must teach us to be more like Christ while on this earth. And who knows; it may even prepare us for some heavenly task the Lord has in store for us.

Living with your wife in an understanding way, while it may not always mean being successful, does mean putting forth the effort, and let's face it, men need the practice. For example, when we hear a radio station playing music sung in a language that we do not understand, at first our brains try to tune in to see if increased volume or focus can increase comprehension. At the point that our brains determine that the station is playing music being sung in a language incomprehensible to it, it shuts down all efforts to interpret the language and considers the radio station to be simply emitting music accompanied by noise. Men frequently do that with their wives. They listen up to the point that they perceive that their spouse is communicating in a way that is incomprehensible to them, at which point they shut down their efforts to understand and either blow up in frustration or retreat into the "silent treatment" that the television provides. When this occurs, women feel hurt and disappointed that the one who should love and care for them the most seems to be completely unconcerned about their feelings, and resentment and bitterness crop up as most women assume this is done out of malice rather than ignorance.

To avoid this problem **most husbands need to develop and hone their listening skills.** Even in situations that men do not completely understand what is being said, listening when their wives speak is ALWAYS valued by women. It communicates that you are concerned about how they feel and what they think enough to try and understand them. There is one bear trap built in these kinds of conversations. In spite of the fact that your wife may ask you for the solution to a problem, she does not always want an answer from you. Sometimes she may just want to vent. As far as I can tell, there are no social clues built into the question to help one tell if it is a genuine question or just an announcement that a lecture on a pet peeve is about to commence. Wise husbands over many years usually learn to tell the difference, mainly by developing their listening skills. As James says, "be quick to hear, slow to speak, and slow to anger" (James 1:19).

Another reason mentioned in 1 Peter 3:7 for living with our wives "in an understanding way" is because she is described as "someone weaker" or "a weaker vessel." While this is generally true of women physically, many women could beat their husband three out of five rounds in the boxing ring. No man who has ever seen his wife in the labor and delivery of a child could reasonably challenge her endurance and toughness. The weaker "vessel" of 1 Peter 3:7, I believe, refers to the ceramic vessels used in the ancient household for virtually every domestic task. Most were inexpensive and expected to break frequently in daily use. Broken pottery forms the basis of the science of modern archeology. Others were "weaker" and used for decorative purposes or more delicate tasks. Fine China can be so thin that light is often seen through it. Because of its fine quality and the fact that it is a "weaker vessel" it must be handled more gently. Therefore, if your wife is 300 pounds and you are a 100 pound weakling, you are still to treat her "as" if she might be easily broken.

Others have tried to attribute a woman's weakness to emotional matters, which while generally true, may have many exceptions in individual marriages we can observe. Even if her emotions are more fragile or volatile than your own, however, as in the physical realm, godly men should treat her as if she were easily broken. She may not be, but God requires that his servants treat her as if she were. But whether the passage discusses physical, emotional, or even theoretical weakness, godly men, especially preachers, must try to understand their wives to the best of their ability. Instead of giving up on it as an impossible task, they keep trying, mostly by being good listeners, but in addition showing her how special she is to you by doing everything to keep from hurting her. Your wife will notice and feel special, and it will be a wonderful silent sermon to others as you serve as a wonderful "example of those who believe" (1 Timothy 4:12).

Examples in Showing Honor to Your Wife

In 1 Peter 3:7b, Peter continues his instruction to husbands: "show her honor as a fellow heir of the grace of life, so that your prayers will not be hindered." Most of the time when we discuss honor or respect it has to do with wives showing proper submission to their husbands. Certainly, given the rise of feminism we must insist that the biblical pattern of the family be taught. This passage, however, is interesting in that it not only commands honor to the wife, but declares that in Christ she is equal (a fellow heir), and points out that it is sinful to fail to treat her with such honor and equality. (What else but sin hinders our prayers?) While we may have different functions, equality between the sexes in Christ is clearly taught here and elsewhere in the New Testament (Galatians 3:26-29). How then can a wife be treated with honor and equality?

Perhaps the best way to honor one's wife is to ensure that she is never dishonored by sexual immorality. As Paul tells the Corinthians in 1 Corinthians 6:18, "Flee fornication" for it is such a dangerous sin to one's body, one's family, and one's soul that the best advice he can give is to RUN! Years later, Paul commands Timothy to "flee from youthful lusts" (2 Timothy 2:22), realizing that nothing can destroy the influence of an evangelist like sexual sin. In our own day, pornography is so commonplace that many men do not consider it as severe as other sexual sins. Internet porn has proven to be as addictive as drugs and may even make initiating sexual activity difficult with real women. [Editors Note – *See the chapter in this book on this subject.*]

One of the best ways to run from sexual sin is to protect yourself from tempting situations or ones in which you could be falsely accused. NEVER meet alone with a woman or with children. Whenever possible make sure your wife is there with you. This shows everyone that you honor her judgment and discretion and that you are a "one woman man" (1 Timothy 3:2).

Treat "the older women as mothers, and the younger women as sisters, in all purity" (1 Timothy 5:2). Paul tells the younger preacher Timothy about his dealings with his sisters in Christ. I truly enjoy the relationship that

I have with my spiritual mothers and sisters. One of the reasons for that is because it is pure and never tainted with a hint of sin or wrong. Also, as a brother/sister relationship it does not give my wife any reason for jealousy, and it does not risk making her feel dishonored in anyway. If my relationship with any Christian, male or female, made my wife feel dishonored or even uncomfortable in any way, I would drop them like a bad habit. My wife needs to be absolutely certain that I value the covenant that we made with each other and that no other friendship or job will stand in the way of my fulfilling the promise I made to my honored wife and partner.

One more issue that I would like to mention briefly is the tendency on the part of many men and even some preachers to insult their wives publicly. It is bad enough to do it privately, but to put-down your spouse in public is sinful according to 1 Peter 3:7. No one likes to be belittled, but to humiliate the one you promised to love and protect lacks all chivalry and godliness. Some say they are just playing, but what else could she say. Once you go down the road of trading insults you never really know if the accuser is serious or teasing or if the accused is hurt or just laughing it off. I do know that an insulted wife is not being honored and a put-down wife is not being treated like an equal heir of eternal life.

> No one likes to be belittled, but to humiliate the one you promised to love and protect lacks all chivalry and godliness.

Examples in Loving Their Wives

The last example I think that should characterize the way all men, but especially gospel preachers, treat their wives is discussed in Ephesians 5:25-33. In this passage husbands are commanded to, "Love your wives, just as Christ also loved the church and gave Himself up for her" (verse 25). Most husbands feel that by marrying their wives they have fulfilled this requirement. However, throughout this instruction to men **the word *agape* is used indicating a love motivated not exclusively by emotions, but by active goodwill toward the one to be loved.** This kind of love does not seek what the beloved can do for you, but how the lover can please the beloved. Think about it! Neither desire, family loyalty, friendship, nor romantic love can be commanded. But in this passage God demands that husbands love their wives, by putting their own welfare beneath their duty to seek what is best for their wives. On top of that, the example used is the way Christ loved the church and "gave Himself up" for it. What an unattainable goal this sounds like! I don't think it is an unattainable goal however, to give oneself for their wives, but one that all godly men and all preachers worthy of the gospel of Christ, will strive to do.

This love is also one that strives to see the wife as holy and blameless rather than constantly seeking to find fault (1 Corinthians 13:5-7). How many marriages break down when wives get fed up with their husbands using them as excuses for everything that goes wrong? Instead husbands are to "love their own wives as their own bodies" (28). If men loved their wives as their own bodies, women would all be treasured.

Real men love their wives, not just by a word here and there or by a present every third year, but by a selfless love that submits your happiness to that of your wife.

Notice how when most men get sick they become worthless and want to be waited on as if certain death were imminent. If a woman is sick, however, she must still do most of her housework tasks and if she is bed-ridden the wheels fall off around the house.

Real men love their wives, not just by a word here and there or by a present every third year, but by a selfless love that submits your happiness to that of your wife. **Gospel preachers should lead the way in loving their wives in this Christ-like manner. Most men have never seen it done.** Evangelists cannot only dispel the notion that a godly marriage is impossible, but by loving their wives as the Scriptures dictate, some good habits may just rub off on those open-minded to the truth.

Conclusion

"Love the Word, love men, and love your wife" may never catch on as a maxim for young preachers like "Know God, and know men." It does not flow in the same poetic manner, nor was it said by some famous preacher to give it credibility or wide circulation as the latter truism. I do believe that it is more complete and features an element that even some of our well known gospel preachers of the past overlooked in their work. Preachers must know and love the Word of God, without which I am convinced they will do more evil than good over their careers. They must also know and love people. Without these skills they will make many social errors, some enemies, misunderstandings, and a few betrayals in their life as preachers. Loving people and their souls keeps one going through the hardships. Loving your wife is a command in Ephesians 5:25-33, and being "an example of those that believe" (1 Timothy 4:12) is commanded of Timothy and expected of all subsequent evangelists. Therefore, brethren, we must do a much better job than we have been doing in this regard. This is not a mild suggestion: God expects scriptural behavior from his servants.

As we have discussed above, 1 Peter 3:7a emphasizes that we must try to understand our wives by listening to them and treating them as if they were easily broken, even if they are not, so they can see how precious and special they are to us. In the last part of verse 7, Peter declares that a failure to honor our wives as equals in the kingdom of God is sinful. This would certainly include making sure that no hint of fornication ever mars your home or dishonors you and your wife. Instead, she should be treated as a valuable partner and confidante in the Lord's work.

Wives should also be loved as Christ loved the church and as men love their own bodies, not by seeking what they can provide for you, but for how you can please and do good toward them. What's more, in all these things, gospel preachers should be the role models and examples in all of these things.

"Love the Word, love men, and love your wife" may not be a phrase that extends beyond this chapter. But if more preachers lived by these three principles, their lives just might be the best sermon that they ever preach.

Works Consulted

Bowman, Dee. **Common Sense Preaching**. Temple Terrace, Florida: Florida College Press, 1999.

Kercheville, Berry. **Preparing the Young Man to Preach**. Lakeland, Florida: Harwell/Lewis Publishing Co., 2005.

Mayer, Jack, Sr. **The Preacher and His Work**. rev.& enl. ed. Shreveport, Louisiana: Lambert Book House, 1960.

Needham, James P. **Preachers and Preaching.** 2nd ed. Brandon, Florida: Bulwarks Bookstore & Bindery, 1985.

[**Editor's postscript:** At the time the chapters for this book were being assembled, Curtis Pope's father (mentioned in the chapter) passed away and his daughter and son-in-law bore Curtis and Mary Ann a grandchild. In addition to our expression of sympathy and congratulation, we offer special appreciation to Curtis for working so well under the pressure of these family events.]

Final Thoughts
Warren E. Berkley

Our primary aim in publishing this book is preventive.

If for some readers it becomes remedial, we will rejoice in individual repentance. The gospel of Christ is God's remedial plan available to penitent sinners willing to activate their faith in the risen Christ. The authors of this book will thank God for those who find the rebuke of sin contained on these pages sufficient to lead them to repentance, or for those who simply make a personal commitment to apply greater diligence and discipline in their thinking and living.

Our priority is prevention. To expose the problems and bring to the pages of this book applicable Bible teaching is intended primarily to prevent the pitfalls that compose the crisis of what has happened behind some preacher's doors. I should like our readers to consider now these final thoughts.

Temptations and struggles with sin place you at a fork in the road of your life. We want this book to help you see the fork and make the right choices before a crisis. We pray you will become heartily engaged in prayer, seek good counsel, repair any damage to the best of your ability and open your eyes to what is best for all who may be involved. The choice is yours. Find the exit off the bad road you have taken. You can choose how to react to your weaknesses, impulses, temptations and opportunities. May those choices be driven by the self-discipline empowered by God's Word inside you.

Please notice that every good course of thought and action recommended in this book requires self-discipline. Reading this book will not suddenly or automatically solve an existing problem, or keep you from future sin. Knowledge must be turned into practice and that is an issue of heart. When it lies in our power to do it, it also lies in our power not to do it (paraphrase, Aristotle).

The problems identified in this book are not limited to any region or generation (except perhaps the new technology that may be used more by the younger generation). It is not about age, inexperience, geography, education, or talent. Men of different ages, young and old, dynamic in the pulpit or "average," known and unknown have exhibited the bad behaviors outlined in this book. While the vast majority of preachers are sincere, righteous and have nothing to hide, a wide variety of men have offended God, betrayed their families, brought churches to crisis, soiled the name of the church to the public and lost their influence. The problem is not limited to a few men who can be specifically described by class or station.

Bro. Bobby Witherington wrote clearly of this over 25 years ago: "… it must be admitted that gospel preachers (also elders) by the score are falling prey to the 'lust of the flesh' (1 John 2:16), are committing fornication against their wives (Matthew 19:9), and even divorcing the morally pure mothers of their children. Notwithstanding the fact that some have preached the gospel for years and have sought to glorify God in their sermons, they are doing the very thing which 'He hateth' (Malachi 2:14-16). They are acting in total opposition to all that they have preached with regards to moral purity and the sanctity of the home. **We are not just referring to a few isolated cases which in the course of a few years' time surface in different parts of the nation. We are referring to a condition which is becoming disgustingly and increasingly more common.** A condition which will send precious souls to hell, and which is adversely affecting both the purity and the growth of that church for which our Savior died." (Emphasis added, -web) [Guardian of Truth XXVIII: 1, pp. 6-7 January 5, 1984]

Every preacher is vulnerable to decline and/or disaster. Anyone can fall. We are not surprised by some, but totally shocked by others. That says it. Anyone can fall. The moment you become convinced you are beyond temptation, at that moment you have opened a door for the devil to gain his entrance. And don't let age and experience deceive you into thinking you have arrived at some untouchable place. Such self-deception can lead to our quick defeat. The mighty can fall, and they do. A sense of humility combined with watchfulness and prayer is a shield and safeguard. "If we think to secure ourselves by prayer only, without watchfulness, we are slothful and tempt God; if by watchfulness, without prayer, we are proud and slight God; and, either way, we forfeit His protection," (Matthew Henry).

A preacher's intelligence, talent, and apparent success does not automatically advantage him before God. The more well known a man is and the better his preaching skills, it seems the greater our shock when he falls. Yet we should know that resistance to temptation is not discovered in those highly visible things so treasured by men. One can know all about the whole armor of God, yet not wear it (Ephesians 6:10-18). It is possible that many have an impressive knowledge base of what the Bible teaches about prayer, but not be a personal participant in prayer. It could be, that some of "our best preachers" in terms of talent, lack the personal discipline to respond faithfully to the subtle temptations arrayed against us. *"Your word I have hidden in my heart, that I might not sin against You,"* *(Psalm 119:11).*

"So then each of us shall give account of himself to God," (Romans 14:12).

Suggested Reading:

Bowman, Dee. *Common Sense Preaching.* Florida College Press, 1999.
Needham, James. *Preachers and Preaching.* Truth Magazine, 1969
Kercheville, Barry. *Preparing the Young Man to Preach.* Harwell-Lewis, 2005.
Petty, Dan (Editor). *Guard the Trust: Studies in Paul's Letters to Timothy and Titus.* FC Lectures, 2009

More Bible workbooks that you can order from Spiritbuilding.com or your favorite Christian bookstore.

BIBLE STUDIES

Inside Out (Carl McMurray)
Studying spiritual growth in bite sized pieces
Night and Day (Andrew Roberts)
Comparing N.T. Christianity and Islam
We're Different Because..., w/Manual (Carl McMurray)
A workbook on authority and recent church history
From Beneath the Altar (Carl McMurray)
A workbook commentary on the book of Revelation
1 & 2 Timothy and Titus (Matthew Allen)
A workbook commentary on these letters from Paul
The Parables, Taking a Deeper Look (Kipp Campbell)
A relevant examination of our Lord's teaching stories
The Minor Prophets, Vol. 1 & 2, w/PowerPack (Matthew Allen)
Old lessons that speak directly to us today
Esteemed of God, the Book of Daniel, w/Manual (Carl McMurray)
Covering the man as well as the time between the testaments
Faith in Action: Studies in James (Mike Wilson)
Bible class workbook and commentary on James
The Lion is the Lamb (Andrew Roberts)
Study of the King of Kings, His glorious kingdom,
& His promised return
Church Discipline, w/Manual (Royce DeBerry)
A quarter's study on an important task for the church
Exercising Authority, w/Manual (John Baughn)
How we use and understand authority on a daily basis
Communing with the Lord (Matthew Allen)
A study of the Lord's Supper and issues surrounding it
Seeking the Sacred (Chad Sychtysz)
How to know God the way that HE wants us to know Him
1 Corinthians & 2 Corinthians study workbooks (Chad Sychtysz)
Detailed studies to take the student through these important letters
Living a Spirit Filled Life, w/PowerPack (Matthew Allen)
An overview study of Galatians & Ephesians with practical applications

TEENS/YOUNG ADULTS

Transitions, w/PowerPack (Ken Weliever)
A relevant life study for twenty-somethings changing age group

**Snapshots: Defining Moments in a Girl's Life
(Nicole Sardinas)**
How to make godly decisions when it really matters

The Path of Peace (Cassondra Givans)
Relevant and important topics of study for teens

The Purity Pursuit (Andrew Roberts)
Helping teens achieve purity in all aspects of life

The Gospel and You (Andrew Roberts)
Thirteen weeks of daily lessons for Jr High and High School ages

Paul's Letter to the Romans (Matthew Allen)
Putting righteousness by faith on an understandable level

WOMEN

Reveal In Me... (Jeanne Sullivan)
A ladies study on finding and developing one's own talents

I Will NOT Be Lukewarm, w/PowerPack (Dana Burk)
A ladies study on defeating mediocrity

The Gospel of John (Cassondra Givans)
A study for women, by a woman, on this letter of John

Sisters at War (Cassondra Givans)
Breaking the generation gap between sisters in Christ

Will You Wipe My Tears? (Joyce Jamerson)
Resources to teach us how to help others through sorrow

Bridges or Barriers, w/Manual (Cindy DeBerry/Angie Kmitta)
Study encouraging harmony with younger/older sisters-in-Christ

Learning to Sing at Midnight (Joanne Beckley)
A study book about spiritual growth benefiting women of all ages

Forgotten Womanhood (Joanne Beckley)
Workbook which covers purity of purpose in serving God

Re-charging Your Prayer Life (Lonnie Cruse)
Workbook for any woman wanting a richer prayer life

Heading for Harvest (Joyce Jamerson)
A study to help ladies digest the fruit of the Spirit

PERSONAL GROWTH
Compass Points (Carl McMurray)
22 foundation lessons for home studies or new Christians
Marriage Through the Ages, w/Manual (Royce & Cindy DeBerry)
A quarter's study of God's design for this part of our life
Parenting Through the Ages, w/Manual (Royce & Cindy DeBerry)
Bible principles tested and explained by successful parents
What Should I Do?, w/Manual (Dennis Tucker)
A study that seeks Bible answers to life's important questions
When Opportunity Knocks, w/Manual (Matthew Allen)
Lessons on how to meet the JW/Mormon who knocks on your door

SPECIAL INTERESTS
In the Eye of the Hurricane - AUTISM (Juli Liske)
A family's journey from the shock of an autistic diagnosis to victory
I Cried Out, You Answered Me - DEPRESSION
(Sheree McMillen)
What happens when faith and depression live in the same home
Her Little Soldier - DIABETES (Craig Dehut)
The journey of a young man suffering from Type 1 Juvenile Diabetes
For However Brief a Time (Warren Berkley)
A son's human interest tales of his father in a time now gone by
Family Bible Study Series (Ken Weliever)
A series of 16 quarters of Bible class curriculum ideas

JUST FOR KIDS
Greta's Purpose (Rebecca Helvey)
A children's book about a Great Dane who struggles with fitting in
Rudy's Path (Rebecca Helvey)
A story of a chocolate colored dog who finds belief,
a family, and a name
Gus and Phil Stories Audio CDs (Ivan Benson)
Stories of true friendship and Christian values
Spiritbuilding Bible Challenge on CD (Mark Hudson, Alayne Hunt)
An entertaining CD-ROM series of Bible questions & answers
*All PowerPacks include PowerPoint presentations + Teacher's Manual

www.ingramcontent.com/pod-product-compliance
Lightning Source LLC
Chambersburg PA
CBHW020041040426
42331CB00030B/118